D0720327

Are you a Super Man?

Becoming God's Man of Steel

By Steve Etner

Learn more about this book
and its author by visiting our web site:
www.overboardministries.com

Copyright © 2017 Overboard Ministries
All rights reserved.
ISBN-10: 1-943635-14-5
ISBN-13: 978-1-943635-14-6

This book is also available as an eBook.
Visit www.overboardministries.com for details.

All Scripture quotations, unless otherwise indicated, are taken from
The Holy Bible, English Standard Version (ESV), copyright © 2001 by
Crossway, a publishing ministry of Good News Publishers. Used by
permission. All rights reserved.

Scripture quotations marked NIV '84 are taken from The Holy Bible,
New International Version. Copyright © 1973, 1978, 1984 by
International Bible Society. Used by permission of Zondervan
Publishing House. All rights reserved.

Scripture quotations marked NKJV are taken from the New King James
Version®. Copyright © 1982 by Thomas Nelson. Used by permission.
All rights reserved.

CONTENTS

Dedication

First, I want to dedicate this book to the men of First Baptist Church of Elkhart, Indiana: specifically, to my Bible Study group. These men faithfully labored through this material with me, helping me define, refine and confine it all into the book you hold in your hand.

To those men I say a never-ending Thank You. Your patience and input was invaluable. Even more, your application of God's truth to your lives as we worked through this study together is what this endeavor is all about!

Second, it is my deep honor to dedicate this book to one man who is a true definition of a Super Man of God. Pastor John Blodgett is not only my pastor, my shepherd, and my spiritual guide; he has also become a dear friend. In the 20-plus years that he has been my pastor, John has consistently and faithfully modeled for me spiritual manhood. He is unwavering in his faith, faithful in his life, and lives in a way that always draws attention to the awesome God he serves. Thank you, Pastor, for pouring your heart and soul into ministering to me!

INTRODUCTION
Meet Our Hero

*Faster than a speeding ticket, more powerful than
the Energizer Bunny, able to leap tall bushes in a
single bound; bends a wet noodle with his bare hands
and changes the course of mighty anthills; and who
—disguised as Mitch, a mild-mannered father of
three and deacon in the church—fights a never-
ending battle for truth, godliness
and the Christian way.*

Our scene opens with Mild-Mannered Mitch sitting in his pastor's office, anxiously wringing his hands while staring blankly out the window. At that moment he feels anything but the superhero he is trying so hard to be. Once again he has encountered his Kryptonite—and this time it has struck a nasty blow.

"I can't believe I did that again!" he sighs. "Pastor, why do I keep doing the things I don't want to do? This isn't supposed to be happening to me! Why do I struggle so much with this stupid habit? Why is this sin haunting me? After everything I've tried, after all the help you've given me, I should be over it by now!"

Sitting behind his desk, silently praying for wisdom—and for Mitch—Pastor watches his friend hang his head in shame. Softly, mournfully Mitch groans, "I hate this sin, so why do I keep giving in to it?"

Can you relate? Can you feel the ache in Mitch's heart? We try to be the super man others want, need, even expect us to be. And, to be honest, most of the time we succeed—at least partially. We do fairly well at presenting the "spiritual man of steel" persona to those around us, yet inwardly we are anything but the men we want to be.

Like Superman, your strength, your ability to effectively live a life that honors and glorifies God, your capacity to stand firm in the faith and fight off the attacks of the enemy and be God's man of steel, comes directly from the Son. The closer you are in your relationship to the Son, Jesus Christ, the greater is your power. You see, it's "His divine power (that) has given us everything we need for life and godliness" (2 Peter 1:3, addition mine).

There are times, those ever so annoying times, that our own personal Kryptonite—the sin that so easily traps us—weakens our will and ability to fight, and typically that's when we give in to temptation. At the moment it feels good, almost rewarding ... almost. But then, once the wave of enjoyment passes over us, we are left sinking in the muck of regret, guilt and even shame. Where once we walked in victory, we now wallow in defeat. Oh, that stupid Kryptonite.

If you're anything like me, after encountering your Kryptonite for the umpteenth time, you begin questioning things. *"Why do I continue to do the things I don't want to do? Why can't I be consistent in living a life that glorifies God? Why can't I get victory once and for all over this sin-issue in my life?"* Don't think you're alone in this, my friend. We are all right there with you. We all encounter nasty pieces of our past that weaken us and undermine us. Even the Apostle Paul significantly wrestled with this issue (in fact, I challenge you to take a moment and read Romans 7:15-25).

Many of us—if not most of us—have even tried to barter and bargain with God in the process. Maybe you've prayed something like this: "Father, if you will only take this away from me, I promise You I will _____ *(fill in the blank with some great and grand gesture on your part, meant to somehow impress God with your magnificent sacrifice)*!" Deuteronomy 10:17 says, "For the Lord your God is God of gods and Lord of lords, the great, the mighty, and the awesome God, who *is not partial and takes no bribe*." Hmmm, why doesn't bartering and bargaining with God work? Why do we even try?

It can be very discouraging when you've cried out to God for forgiveness, mercy and grace to help in your time of need—only to find that just a few short hours (or if you're lucky, days) later, that persistent piece of your past once again pops up, weakening your will and ability to fight. You fall back into that same old sinful routine. The overwhelming feelings of guilt and shame drive you down to your knees in a renewed resolve to *never* do that again. Yet the very next day, the cycle repeats itself. Over and over, you continuously give in to the same temptations that relentlessly pound you down. Oh, that stupid Kryptonite.

For many of us, this self-defeating pattern can leave us wondering, *"What's wrong with me?"* Maybe you've even found yourself blame-shifting by asking, *"What's wrong with God? Why is He failing me? Why isn't He helping me? Why can't I change? God, why won't you change me?"*

Pause here for a moment and consider this: it's not that we "can't" change, nor is it that for some cosmic, unknown reason the Almighty, all-powerful God of the Universe is choosing not to change us; but rather that, deep down, we don't want to change.

Say what? Seriously, dude—way down in the core of our beings we don't want to change. We like our sinful habits. We enjoy the pleasures that life on this planet provides. And so, even though we make the occasional attempt at changing, even though we "try" to turn our lives around, nothing happens. No real, lasting change takes place.

You see, we do what we do because in our hearts we want what we want. If life is about *my* pleasure and *my* happiness, then it only makes sense that I will focus on doing those things that I think will help me achieve *my* goals.

It is vitally important that we get this concept, or this study will be pointless. As long as King Me is sitting on the throne of my heart, everything I think, say and do will be for the benefit of King Me! That's our Kryptonite. That's the one thing that constantly gets between us and the Son. That is what drains us of our supernatural ability to stand firm against the attacks of the enemy. King Me needs to come off the throne of our lives, finally and for good!

God has promised to equip us with everything we need to live a life that honors him—to be His Man of Steel (read 2 Peter 1:3). However, if real change is going to happen, if we are going to be the Super Men that God has called us to be, we must daily (moment by moment) choose to remove the "I" from life—dethroning and deposing King Me.

Guys, stop hanging around and playing around with your Kryptonite! The bottom line is simple: the outer man (my human behavior) will not consistently glorify God until the inner man (my heart, my spiritual being) learns to glorify Him every moment of every day.

So here we go: face the Son, identify your Kryptonite, and let's become God's Men of Steel!

Steve Etner

*"So whether you eat or drink or whatever you do,
do it all for the glory of God."*
1 Corinthians 10:31

Week #1
Are You a Super Man?

Week 1, Day 1

Alright, guys, let's face it: life can be confusing, even frustrating at times! C'mon, admit it. You think you're doing okay, coasting along fairly smoothly. You believe you're making the right choices. In fact, at times you feel like you could rip open your shirt and reveal that big red **S** on the center of your chest. You feel on top of your game, nearly indestructible, and safe. You're almost convinced everything is going to be alright when suddenly—Kryptonite! It comes out of nowhere, and you get slammed hard. Been there, right? Not fun.

You're trying to do everything right, to be a Super Man of God:

- You're having your personal devotions.
- You're trying to be consistent in your prayer life.
- You painstakingly struggle through Scripture memory.
- You're going to church every week.
- You faithfully put your offering in the plate as it's passed.
- And even though poopy diapers just ain't your thing, you're serving in the nursery department complete with rubber gloves, a clothespin on your nose, and a smile on your face.
- You lead your family in devotions.
- You massage your wife's feet.
- You even help out by folding your own clean underwear.

In spite of all that, the job seems to have stalled; you've been passed up once again for that promotion. The economy has taken yet another turn for the worse. Your house was broken into while you were out

1

buying the third pair of shoes for the kids this year (and it's only May). The car conked out on you just two blocks from home. Gas prices are climbing—again; the electric bill has skyrocketed; the refrigerator just died, leaving a puddle on the floor that is now leaking into the basement; and you have to run a child to the hospital to get a bone set and cast. Oh, and the pretty neighbor lady is sunbathing in a skimpy bikini right outside your bathroom window. Stressed and discouraged, you toss your hands up in the air and shout, "There's got to be more to life than this, right? Otherwise, what's the point?"

Hey, it's tough being a Super Man of God!

Solomon's Solemn Scene
Let me introduce you to a man in the Bible named Solomon. I'm sure you've heard of him. He's the guy who asked God to give him a boatload of wisdom. He's the guy who had King David as a father and Bathsheba as his mom. He's the guy who wrote the books of Proverbs and Song of Solomon. He's the guy who built a magnificent temple to the Lord. Oh, and he's also the guy who had 700 wives and 300 concubines—not so sure about the wisdom in that decision.

In the Old Testament book of Ecclesiastes, Solomon tells the story of his massive quest to find a sense of purpose and meaning to his life. Let me lay out the plotline for you. Bored and frustrated, Solomon utilized his position and power, along with every resource he could get his hands on, in an attempt to find happiness and significance. Yet no matter how much money he put in the bank, how many things he accumulated, how many friends he made or how many different types of pleasures he pursued, he wasn't happy. It just wasn't enough. He couldn't find true meaning to his life.

In fact, at one point in his search, exhausted and discouraged, he pulled out his journal, sharpened his quill, dipped it in ink and summarized his feelings of emptiness by writing, "I have seen all the things that are done under the sun; all of them are meaningless, a chasing after the wind" (Ecclesiastes 1:14). Have you ever felt that way? Have you ever wondered at the end of the day, *"What's the point? Why bother with this endless, mind-numbing routine?"*

A few years earlier King David, Solomon's father, experienced the exact same frustrations. David summarized it this way: "Man is a mere phantom as he goes to and fro: He bustles about, but only in vain; he heaps up wealth, not knowing who will get it" (Psalm 39:6). Wow. What kind of a life is that? Doesn't that sound satisfying? *"Hey, put all your time, energy, attention and effort into acquiring lots of stuff, because in the end it won't be yours anyway!"* Sure makes me want to swing my feet out of bed in the morning, how about you?

One might hope that Solomon would learn a valuable lesson from dear ol' dad. *"Son, it's just not worth it to pursue life without God. Stuff won't make you happy—trust me, I know!"* But Solomon, like so many of us, chose not to listen. He had to learn the hard way. Always the hard way.

Near the end of his search, frustrated with his lack of results, it begins to dawn on Solomon that he has wasted his life by looking in all the wrong places. I can just see him in the palace, sitting on a throne inlaid with gold and decked out with all kinds of precious stones and jewels. He is surrounded by dignitaries who have come from all over just to pick his brain in the hopes of hearing some great, wise tidbit fall from his lips. Sighing, he rises from the throne and strolls past the large, hand-carved cedar doors leading to his extensive library. Once outside, deep in thought, he ignores the beauty and grandeur of the massive, unparalleled garden he recently had built, and continues past the winery.

Walking down the winding path toward the lower pool, he hears his friends laughing and having a grand time. Wanting to be alone with his musings, he turns away and strolls along a path surrounded by blooming asphodel, hyssop and blue lupines. The pungent scent of the flowers and the multicolored butterflies flitting from blossom to blossom are lost on him as he agonizes over his thoughts.

Stopping at the edge of one of his orchards, he plucks a fruit from the nearest tree. His teeth sink deep with a crisp snap, and the juice flows freely down his beard. However, in his melancholy the exquisite taste is lost on him. He stands for a moment, head cocked to one side, listening to the bleating of his large flock of sheep off in the distance. He can just see, over the top of the trees, a glint of gold as the setting sun shines off the cupola of his enormous treasury. A faint sound of giggling briefly jerks him out of his deep thoughts. As the conversation grows louder, a small group of women from his harem walk past him, smiling as they go by. He doesn't smile back.

Standing there, Solomon comes to the stark realization that spending his life trying to find *things* that would make him happy did not produce the results he had anticipated. After all he had done, after all he had accumulated, and after everything he had accomplished, he was still coming up empty-handed. All those things and all those accomplishments didn't make him the Super Man he thought he would be.

Back in his private chambers, he pulls out his journal and makes this final, powerful entry. "Now all has been heard; here is the conclusion of the matter: Fear God and keep His commandments, for this is the whole duty of man" (Ecclesiastes 12:13). Laying down the quill, he sits back, folds his arms across his chest, slowly shakes his head in frustration, and just stares at those words. How has he been so foolish?

Solomon could have saved himself a lot of heartache and frustration, if only he had started his quest with God instead of self. Could it be that there's a lesson here for us to learn as well? We could certainly save ourselves that same heartache and frustration if we would just listen to Solomon's wisdom and the experience of his father David. To be a Super Man of God, start with God instead of King Me.

Give it Some Thought
- Read the following verses, and make a list of all the things Solomon chased after just to find some meaning in his life (Ecclesiastes 1:13, 16-17; 2:1-10).

- Read Ecclesiastes 1:14 and 2:11, 17. What did Solomon liken those things to, and why?

- Why was Solomon's search for purpose and meaning to life ultimately unsuccessful?

- Name some of the things you have seen guys try (or you have personally tried) outside of God in order to find purpose and meaning to life.

  - Which of those things are "bad," and what makes them bad?

- Why do we spend so much time and energy on "things" instead of on what truly matters?

- Read Matthew 16:23-26 and Galatians 1:10. In what ways has King Me been on the throne of your heart?

Week 1, Day 2

The Purpose of Purpose

One of our greatest challenges as men is to find some sort of purpose to life. Guys want to know they're important, significant and needed. Guys want to be appreciated; we want to feel—well, we want to feel manly. Without a sense of direction and a feeling of significance, men tend to wander (physically, mentally, emotionally and even spiritually). Usually we will withdraw to our safe place, our go-to spot, that thing or place that makes us feel like men (insert an appropriate man-grunt here).

For some guys, it's sports. Football, basketball, baseball, hockey, hunting, fishing, you name it. For others, it's cars. Let them tinker under the hood for a while and they're as happy as a tick on a lazy dog. Some guys choose to sit in front of their entertainment device of choice (be it X-box, Playstation, the computer, or whatever) and try to just zone out for a couple of hours. And let's be honest, for some guys it's porn, or alcohol, drugs or cigarettes.

---

2 Timothy 1:9

"(God) saved us and called us to a holy calling, not because of our works but because of his own purpose and grace, which he gave us in Christ Jesus before the ages began."

Gentlemen, I challenge you to pause long enough to consider this fact: you were created for one purpose alone, and that is to know God and live a life that brings honor and glory to Him in everything you think, everything you say and everything you do.[1] It's only when you are living out that God-given purpose that you will find real significance.

God created you for a reason. You were designed by the Almighty to glorify Him. It's programmed within your very DNA! It's at the very heart of who you are as a man. Whatever you do, whenever you do it, wherever you are as you're doing it, you are to always and at all times do it in Jesus' name[2] and for his glory.[3] Live like that, and you will indeed be a Super Man of God.

Think about it this way: the object of a football game is to score a touchdown (or field goal) while keeping the other team from doing the same. All 22 players know exactly why they are on the field. They know what their position and purpose is, they know what is expected of them, what is at stake, and they know what they should be doing every moment the game clock is ticking and the ball is in play.

The object of a basketball game is to get the ball into the basket while preventing your opponent from doing the same. All ten players on the court know this. As a result, each team member is playing the game with purpose and direction. He has a specific objective in mind. If he didn't, he would be wandering around aimlessly on the court, getting in everyone's way. Truth be told, he wouldn't be playing for very long.

So, what exactly is the object of life? What's the purpose of having a sense of purpose? What is the point of being a Super Man of God? When you were conceived, the Maker[4] knew exactly what He was creating. He knew why He created you, and what *you*—as His creation—are supposed to do in life. You have been designed for a specific reason and purpose. Until you discover what that purpose is (spoiler alert: it's living a life that honors and glorifies Him), and then determine to live out that purpose every day of your life, you will always be seeking, never able to find fulfillment, meaning and satisfaction.

When you aren't living a life that honors God, when you aren't doing what God created you to do, you experience a big hole in your heart. You have felt it; I know you have. Something is missing. You end up wandering through life trying to find it, trying to make sense of it all. Solomon felt that hole and spent most of his life attempting to fill it with anything and everything but God. Nothing worked! Why? Because nothing—absolutely nothing—can take the place of God! Only God is God, and only He can fill that God-hole in your life.

Psalm 25:4-5

"Make me to know your ways, O Lord; teach me your paths. Lead me in your truth and teach me, for you are the God of my salvation; for you I wait all the day long."

The real question here is this: Are you doing what God created you to do? Are you fulfilling your purpose in life? Isaiah asks the question, "Why spend your labor on what does not satisfy?" (Isaiah 55:2). Think about that. Why do you do some of the things you're doing, when in the long run they don't satisfy? If it doesn't bring honor and glory to God, why are you doing it?

Let me encourage you from the get-go to take your eyes off those things that cannot satisfy, and put your laser-like focus completely on living a super-powerful life that glorifies God.

Solomon started with self and ended with God. May I suggest that we learn from his mistake and just remove self from the equation altogether? Simply start with God! I don't want to see you get to the end of your life and say, "I have labored to no purpose; I have spent my strength in vain and for nothing" (Isaiah 49:4).

Give it Some Thought
- As a man, what is your primary purpose in life, and why? (See 1 Corinthians 10:31 and Colossians 3:17 for help.)

- Think about your answer. As a man, what are some practical ways you can live out that purpose in your daily life?

- Typically, what is your safe place, your go-to spot when you feel frustrated, stressed or otherwise out-of-sorts?

- Why? What does that do for you?

- Why are "things" unable to provide us with true meaning and purpose? (See Luke 12:15 for help.)

  - Why do we turn to things instead of to God?

- According to Matthew 6:33, what should be our priority in life?

  - How are you doing with that?

  - How can we as a group of men help you with that?

- If we followed Solomon's advice in Ecclesiastes 12:13, what do you think would happen?

Week 1, Day 3

Do You Really Want to be a Super Man?
Silly question, right? I know. I mean, what guy doesn't want to be a superman? But humor me for a moment and try to answer it honestly. I'm serious now. Don't just flippantly take a swing at this. Think deep. Think long and think hard. Concentrate. *Make* the bat connect with the ball.

Do you want to be a Super Man of God? Do you truly *want* to live a life that consistently glorifies God? Do you *want* to be God's Man of Steel? Deep down in your gut, do you want, long for, desire, and crave a life totally characterized by godliness, no matter what?

- Write your answer here:

I'm going to assume that your answer is something like this: *"Yes. I want to live a life that in every way reflects God. I want to daily be, think, do, say, and feel in the ways God wants me to. I genuinely want to glorify God in every part of my life!"* To that I stand up and shout "Great!" By the way, I actually did stand up and shout—freaked out my dog, but I did it for you, bro. However, my follow-up question for you then is this: Why? Why do you want to be a Super Man of God?
- Write your answer here:

Your answer to the above question is important, my friend. The motivation of your heart for living a life that glorifies God will make all the difference in the world. If you are trying to be a Super Man of God so *you* can be victorious over the enemy, so *you* can be the kind of guy that others look up to, so *you* can be a spiritual leader in your church, then you have the wrong motivation.

- Read the following verses: Proverbs 16:2; James 4:3; Galatians 1:10; 1 Thessalonians 2:4. What does God say about your motivation?

Don't misunderstand me here. Yes, you need to be victorious over the enemy, and it's a great thing to be a spiritual leader in your church. But if that's your reasoning for becoming a Super Man of God, you've placed the emphasis upon yourself, not God.

Our goal here is to be the kind of men who honor God in everything we think, say and do. Every moment of every day. So, what are you doing *right now* to achieve that goal? C'mon—man to man—what plan of action do you have in place right now to pursue God's purpose for your life? What steps are you taking to be God's Man of Steel, and whom have you asked to hold you accountable?

- Write your answer here—but be sure to write in present tense, "I am"—and be honest:

Turning the "Want To" into a "Will Do"
Wanting to be God's Man of Steel is a great first step. In fact, when your heart's motivation for wanting to be godly is correct (honoring God with your life) you're well on your way to success! However, simply wanting something isn't going to make it happen. For example, at the time of this writing I want to be 20 pounds lighter (sadly, my

Superman T doesn't look all that impressive with a big blue bulge in the middle and hairy belly poking out at the bottom). Unless I change my daily life habits and consistently adhere to a specific diet and exercise program, losing weight and showing off my 4½-pack isn't going to happen (at my age anything greater than a two-pack is sayin' something). In fact, if I'm not careful, just the opposite could happen.

You may *want* to be a godly man, but unless you make some spiritual lifestyle changes, you won't see your desire transform into reality— and that's a fact. So consider this next point very carefully. God stands ready to help you become a man of steel. He wants you to be a Super Man of God. But He also wants to be the One who gets the glory. Taking a stand against the enemy, resisting him in the power of Christ, is an incredible opportunity to give honor and praise to the only One who gives you the strength to do so.

So again, I ask you, what are you doing *right now* to pursue godliness?

Give it Some Thought
- Why do we try so hard to present the image of a Super Man to others?

- Who do you know that could be characterized as a Super Man of God?

- What characteristics set him apart as being a godly man?

- Read Deuteronomy 10:12-13. What are the five characteristics of God's Man of Steel?

- Take a few moments as a group to discuss what each of those characteristics mean, and how to apply them to your life.

Week 1, Day 4

What Do You Know?

Do you know Michael Jordan? I'm talkin' about one of the most amazing pro basketball players of the 20th century. Do you know Michael Jordan?

For example, did you know that he led the Chicago Bulls to six NBA championships and won the MVP (Most Valuable Player) Award five times? Did you know he was born on February 17, 1963, in Brooklyn, New York, but grew up in Wilmington, North Carolina? Okay, how about the fact that he won Olympic gold medals in 1984 and 1992, tried his hand at baseball with the Chicago White Sox, came back to basketball in 1995 and was named one of the 50 greatest players in NBA History by the NBA? Those are a lot of great facts about MJ. But that's all they are, nothing but facts. None of them help us to really *know* Michael.

Do you know the God of this Universe? Do you know Elohim? Facts and figures about God are all great and good, but knowing a lot of details about your Creator isn't necessarily going to help you live a godly life. It's not going to help you stand firm against the attacks of your enemy when he tries to take you down.

If all you have is an intellectual understanding of God, the only thing you will have gained is a lot of great head knowledge (and the ability to win hands down at Bible Trivia games). We need to get to know God much deeper than a bunch of facts and figures. We need to know our Heavenly Father far more than just the few Bible verses we memorized in Sunday School.

- When your efforts are focused only on increasing your knowledge of the Bible, you run the risk of centering your life on works instead of a relationship. You will find Christianity to be more of a burden instead of a blessing. Why?

As we truly get to know God on an intimate level, we will *trust* Him with more control of our lives. Only as we surrender ourselves and yield our lives to God will we become God's Men of Steel.

Jesus loved sticking it to the religious leaders of the day. On one occasion, He said something like this to them: "Oh, you guys really think you're something, don't you! You diligently study the Scriptures because you think that by your deep knowledge of the original language, and your awesome ability to parse verbs and identify dangling participles, you possess eternal life. Seriously? C'mon guys, you're smarter than this! The Scriptures you are studying are the very words that tell you all about Me. Yet you refuse to give up your priestly piety and pompous pride so that you can come to me to have life." (See John 5:39-40.)

Oh, those guys were intent on learning and knowing Scriptures, yes; but their hearts' motivation was all wrong. Their focus was on gaining knowledge of the Word of God for the sake of knowledge itself. They believed their followers were going to be impressed with their ability to understand, interpret and apply God's Word—even if they were applying it in a wrong way.

For them it was all about King Me looking good and sounding all holy and super saintly. It wasn't about God. They put so much value on their head-knowledge that they totally missed the Son of God—the One whom the Bible is about—the One who was standing right before them. Jesus was verbally grabbing them by the collars of their sanctimonious robes and shouting, "These are the Scriptures that testify about *me*!"

Do you have a head knowledge of the Word of God, but not a heart relationship with the God of the Word? You can know a lot of great Biblical truths and principles; you can have a lot of Scripture verses memorized and know Bible doctrine; but if you are not living out those truths in your daily life, if you are not *living* by the doctrine you know to be true, you are not glorifying God—you are not a Super Man of God. Period.

So, let me ask you this:

- What excites God?
- What angers Him?
- What concerns Him?
- What makes Him sad?
- How much does He love you, and in what ways does He show it?
- What are His deepest desires for you?
- What does he want for your life?
- How does He want you to live and work and play?

That's the kind of knowledge we need. That's the kind of knowledge that will draw you closer to him and enable you to stand firm against the enemy. However, that kind of knowledge doesn't come from knowing a bunch of Bible verses and doctrine. It comes only as you invest time with your Creator, daily. As you discover who God really is, your heart will begin to change toward Him. Your focus will wean off of self and will be increasingly placed on loving the One who eternally loves you!

Give it Some Thought
- Why do we so often try to achieve godliness in our own strength?

- Read Jeremiah 9:23-24 and 2 Peter 3:18. How does someone get to know God?

- Read Proverbs 3:5-6; Psalm 28:7 and 37:4-6. Why do we struggle with trusting God totally and completely?

- What does knowing and trusting God have to do with being a Super Man?

Week 1, Day 5

Plan the Act – Act the Plan
On day three you were asked, "What are you doing *right now* to pursue godliness?" Consider carefully the use of the words "right now" in that question.

A plan of action is just a plan until you put it into action. I know; profound, right? The best-laid plan is totally worthless until you *do* something about it. No action? It's just a plan. It may be a good plan, maybe even a great plan, but until you do something about it, it's accomplishing nothing.

If you wait till tomorrow to act, it's just a plan. If you wait till you have an accountability partner to help you, it's still just a plan. If you wait until you purchase that really awesome Bible study software or latest book, it's nothing more than a plan. In fact, I'll go so far as to say that no matter what the reason, if you wait to do something about your pursuit of godliness, it's a plan that has failed. Why? Because you're not acting upon it. Let me say it again: a plan of action is just a plan until you put it into action.

> ### Psalm 119:1-5
>
> *"Blessed are those whose way is blameless, who walk in the law of the Lord! Blessed are those who keep his testimonies, who seek him with their whole heart, who also do no wrong, but walk in his ways! You have commanded your precepts to be kept diligently. Oh that my ways may be steadfast in keeping your statutes!"*

If you wait till tomorrow to act, it's just a plan. If you wait till you have an accountability partner to help you, it's still just a plan. If you wait until you purchase that really awesome Bible study software or latest book, it's nothing more than a plan. In fact, I'll go so far as to say that no matter what the reason, if you wait to do something about your pursuit of godliness, it's a plan that has failed. Why? Because you're not acting upon it. Let me say it again: a plan of action is just a plan until you put it into action.

If we are going to *be* godly men, if we are going be Super Men who live consistently in a way that truly honors God, then we must understand it's not going to happen simply because we want it to.

"Just add the Holy Spirit and—'poof'—you're godly." Nope, doesn't work that way. Nor does godliness come easily. *"Follow these ten easy steps and you'll be a Super Man of God!"* Unh-unh. Godliness is a process combining both faith and action. We must intentionally train ourselves to be godly.[7]

My present physique is more "eek" than it is "phys." I just can't seem to lose my few extra pounds and get into shape. I realize it just might have something to do with the fact that I sit in my office all day and on the couch all evening; and I suppose my eating habits don't necessarily contribute to my overall wellbeing—but c'mon, for a guy in the prime of life, I'm doing pretty well. I have a treadmill, a stationary bike, a great pair of running shoes, and a really cool pair of shorts and t-shirt that are color coordinated. I even have a MP3 player with great running music and a nice pair of earbuds that fit comfortably in my ears! Oh, and get this (dramatic drumroll please), I even have a set of weights!

Impressed? You shouldn't be. You see, even though I have all those things, and even though each of those items can be used to help me achieve my goal of being in shape, they are all worthless. They accomplish nothing if I don't use them.

Paul says that "physical training is of some value, but godliness has value for all things" (1 Timothy 4:8). Did you catch that? There is tremendous value in being a godly man. Great—I'm all about value, so sign me up! Umm, how exactly do I become godly? What's the secret to being God's Man of Steel? The answer, Paul says, is in the training.[8] Oh. Training, huh? You mean I have to actually *do* something in order to be a godly man? Yep. Not just do it, but do it right and do it consistently.

Do you want to be a Super Man of God? Do you want to be stronger spiritually, able to stand firm when the enemy attacks, capable of not giving in to your Kryptonite, bending your will so it conforms to God's? Do you want to be faster, able to go immediately to God when facing a trial or temptation? Do you want to see through the walls of doubt and fear and comprehend what God's path is for your life? Then you must train yourself to be godly.

Give it Some Thought
- What are some practical ways a guy can train himself to be godly?

- Read James 5:16; 1 Thessalonians 5:11; and Ecclesiastes 4:9-12. What role does accountability play in this?

- Name some things you've tried in the past to help yourself become a godly man. What have you found to be successful, and what failed?

- Share with the guys at least one takeaway you received from this week, and what you plan to do about it.

*"I looked for a man among them who would build up the wall and
stand before me in the gap ... but I found none."*
Ezekiel 22:30 NIV '84

Week 2
The Characteristics of God's Man of Steel

Week 2, Day 1

A long time ago, in a galaxy far, far away ... Oh, wait a minute—
wrong story. It does seem like ages ago I was a kid wearing a red bath
towel clothes-pinned around my neck, running through the back yard,
super-cape flapping behind me, pretending to be Kal-El—better
known as Superman—from the Planet Krypton.

Back then, almost every boy I knew secretly wished he could be that
man of steel. And why wouldn't we? After all, Superman had
awesome superpowers. He could fly, he was faster than a speeding
bullet, he was practically invulnerable, he had x-ray vision (how cool
is that), and he always beat the bad guy. He was my hero.

Today I am older and more mature (I only wear my Superman cape on
the first Thursday night of every month—standing in front of a fan in
my basement, hands on my hips and chin held high), but I still
secretly wish I could be a man of steel. Although I no longer have
aspirations of flight, ultra-speed or the ability to see through walls
(though I still think that would be pretty cool), I do long to be a man
of God who stands for Truth, righteousness and the godly way. I want
to be the one who always beats the bad guy.

A Super Man's Power Source
In the DC Comics series about Superman, we discover that he draws
supernatural powers from one single source—Earth's sun. Without the
energy from the sun he is just a normal being, like everyone else.

Without the sun, he has no supernatural abilities. Without the sun, he cannot defeat the enemy. Simply put, without the sun, he's just not Superman.

Spiritually speaking, for you and me to be Super Men of God we must also tap in to a very specific power source. You see, our ability to be God's Men of Steel, our capacity to stand firm and fight off all the attacks of the enemy—the strength we have to be Super Men of God —comes directly from the *Son*. The fact is, it is only through Christ that we can do anything for God; because Christ alone gives us the strength to do it.[1]

> ## 2 Peter 1:3
> *"His divine power has granted to us all things that pertain to life and godliness, through the knowledge of him who called us to his own glory and excellence."*

Without the Son, we are powerless. Without the Son, we cannot stand firm in the faith. Without the Son, we are incapable of defeating the enemy. Bottom line: apart from the Son, we can do nothing.[2] The closer we grow in our relationship with Jesus Christ, the greater our ability to be strong and courageous, to not be frightened and lose heart.[3] As James writes, only when we submit ourselves to God can we effectively resist the Devil and see him turn tail and run like a whipped pup.[4]

You see, guys, no matter how hard we try at being godly men, as long as *we* are the ones trying to be godly, we will be nothing more than just men *trying* to be godly. If I am attempting to be a godly man in my own strength, if I am trying to act out all the things I believe to be the marks and characteristics of godliness by myself, then simply by virtue of the fact that *I'm the one trying to do it*, I will ultimately fail. In our own strength we will never succeed, never achieve and never be Super Men of God.

"You may say to yourself, 'My power and the strength of my hands have produced (this godliness) for me.' But remember the Lord your God, for it is he who gives you the ability to produce (godliness)" (Deuteronomy 8:17-18, additions mine). Truth be told, my friend, you just ain't got the power! You don't have the ability within yourself to be a godly man.

Clothes-pinning a red bath towel around my neck did not make me Superman. Putting on a suit and tie on a Sunday and walking into the church with my Bible tucked under my arm does not make me a godly man. Our ability to be godly men can only come from God, because only God can be godly (look at 2 Corinthians 3:5).

It is "(God's) divine power (that) has granted to us all things that pertain to life and godliness, through the knowledge of him who called us to his own glory and excellence" (2 Peter 1:3). Wow! Did you catch that? The only way we can achieve spiritual Super Man-hood is through the divine power God has chosen to provide us. That power gives us *everything* we need to be godly men.

I've got to repeat that. This is so potent I don't want you to miss it. God has already given you everything you need to live a godly life that honors and glorifies Him! So what's keeping you from being a Super Man of God?

Give it Some Thought
- Who was your hero when you were growing up, and why?

- Other than Jesus, who is your favorite Bible character, and why?

- Read Micah 6:8; James 4:8; and John 15:5. We are to "abide" in Christ, growing in our relationship with Him. What are some ways we, as men, can get closer to the Son?

  - What's hindering us from a closer relationship with God?

- Read 2 Corinthians 12:9. Discuss as a group how God's power is made perfect in your weakness.

- Why would Paul boast in his weakness? How can/should we boast in our weaknesses?

  - How does weakness make us stronger?

Week 2, Day 2

Over 200 years ago, a really smart British dude by the name of Edmund Burke said that the only thing necessary for evil to triumph, was for good men to do nothing.[5] Over 2,000 years ago God spoke to us through an amazing prophet from the Middle East by the name of Ezekiel, and said, "I looked for a man ... who would build up the wall and stand before me in the gap ... but I found none" (Ezekiel 22:30).

Gentlemen, I submit to you that God is still looking for godly men who will choose to stand in the gap and do something great for Him. He's searching for men who will stand with the confidence and power that only God can give and resist the enemy. He's looking for men of steel. He's looking for you—yes, you.

For the rest of this week we are going to look at three super men of God. Three men of steel. Three men who knew what it meant to stand in the gap, square up against the enemy and watch God win the battle.

---

1 Samuel 16:7

"The Lord said to Samuel, 'Do not look on his appearance or on the height of his stature, because I have rejected him. For the Lord sees not as man sees: man looks on the outward appearance, but the Lord looks on the heart.'"

As we begin, let me take a moment and set the stage for you. The books of First and Second Samuel are all about the Kingdom of Israel. Specifically, they focus on a guy named Samuel the Prophet, and the impact he had upon that kingdom. The part of the story we need to focus on here is the fact that King Saul had just disobeyed God. He chose to do his own thing instead of following God's will.[6] As a result, God no longer accepted Saul's leadership as King of His people.[7]

- Why do you think Saul made that choice?

God then instructs Samuel to travel south to a little town called Bethlehem, where he would find a guy named Jesse. Why? Because one of Jesse's eight boys was to become the next King of Israel. Samuel packs his bags, loads up his donkey hatchback and sets off on a little royal road trip.

That's My Boy!

Proud as a daddy could be, knowing why the prophet was in his home, Jesse lined up his sons, youngest to eldest, then stood back—arms folded across his chest, a smile spread from ear to ear. Which boy would it be? Oh, he could hear the neighbors now. He'd be the talk of the town. People from all over would flock to meet the new King of Israel—his son, the King!

Jesse nodded his head in approval as he watched Samuel begin with his eldest, Eliab. After circling him twice, looking him up and down, assessing his physical stature, Samuel began the interview process. At each question, Eliab was quick with an intelligent and sophisticated response. This greatly impressed Samuel. "I believe we've found the next King of Israel," he thought.

The voice in his head nearly made him jump out of his skin. "No, Samuel," God said. "I understand why you think that, but all you can see is the outward appearance. I see much deeper. I look on the heart. I see what you cannot see. I see what motivates a man—and based on what his heart is telling me, I have rejected him. He will not be your next King."[8] Reluctantly Samuel moved on to the next son. And then the next. Seven sons. Seven interviews. Seven times God said, "No."

After he was done questioning the last son, Samuel stepped back and surveyed the line of boys. How could this be? He had undeniably heard God say he was to go to the house of Jesse. That guy standing in the corner with an extremely bewildered look on his face was definitely Jesse. And these were all his boys. Wait a moment. Were they? Could there be any more?

Jesse looked a bit surprised at Samuel's inquiry. His sons passed questioning glances between them. "Well," Jesse responded. "We have a ruddy little runt out in the field babysitting the sheep, but he's just—" "Go get him," Samuel interrupted. "We will go no further until he stands before me," and then Samuel sat down, closed his eyes and waited. The moment young David walked in the door, God said to Samuel, "That's your King!"[9]

In time, David would be described as a man after God's own heart.[10] At that moment, he was merely a young boy who had just been anointed King. God wanted to take some time in David's life to prepare him for what was ahead. So God sent David out to kill a Philistine giant named Goliath.[11] That astonishing victory skyrocketed David into the public eye as a mighty warrior, and he was put in charge of all of Saul's army.[12] In fact, David got so much recognition that the women began to sing songs about how Saul had killed his thousands, but David had killed his tens of thousands.[13]

Now that royally ticked off Saul. He was so jealous, and so angry, that he tried to kill David more than once. David fled to the hills to save his life. It's important you understand: that's exactly where God wanted David to be. You see, it was there in those hills, it was there as he was fearing for his life, it was there as he was doubting the hand of God, that David met up with a band of men who would eventually be known as David's mighty men of valor—God's men of steel.

Imagine for a moment that you are David. You're scared to death. You just dodged yet another spear meant to separate head from neck. Fearing for your life, you split, you skedaddle, you head for the hills. You find a remote cave and you hunker down and hide. You cry out to God for help. *"God, what are you doing? I thought I was to be King! It's not supposed to be like this! God, I don't understand. God, help me!"*

And what does God do? He brings you a rag-tag group of 400 men who are distressed, discontented and in debt. A bunch of messed up dudes.[14] And yet, those were the guys God hand-selected to be David's mighty men. Those were the guys God chose to be His men of steel.

Even today, the men God chooses to use are just normal, ordinary, everyday guys. Would you say that's a fairly accurate description of you? Would you agree that you are just a normal, ordinary, everyday guy? On their own, David's band of brothers weren't men of steel. On their own they were just guys with problems, guys with chips on their shoulders, guys who had made some bad choices in life and were paying the consequences.

But God brought them together in the wilderness, and God began to work in their hearts. As He worked on their hearts, they began to yield to the lordship and leadership of the Almighty, all-powerful God of the Universe in their lives. That is when they became God's Men of Steel.

Let's face it, guys: many of us struggle with feeling distressed and discontented, and most of us are in debt. On our own we aren't mighty men. On our own we're just guys with problems, guys with chips on our shoulders, guys who have made some bad decisions in life and are paying the consequences.

Yet God has brought us together. And as we live together in the middle of a wicked, sinful world, God is working on our hearts. As God is working on *your* heart, what are *you* going to do with what He's accomplishing? Will you choose to totally yield to His lordship and leadership in your life? Will you let Him make you into a Super Man of God?

Give it Some Thought

- Point to Ponder: man looks on the outward appearance, but God looks on your heart. Which aspect of your life do you tend focus upon—your exterior (physical pleasure), or your interior (spiritual growth)? Why?

- Which is more important? Why?

- We saw that Saul chose to do his own thing instead of following God's will. He's not the only one, is he? Why do we tend to do that, too?

- Read 1 Samuel 15:1-34. Why was God so angry with Saul's disobedience?

  - How do you think God feels when you choose to disobey Him? Why?

- Why do men tend to want to "do life" alone—why don't we like to "go deep" with other guys?

  - What do the following passages have to say about that? Ecclesiastes 4:9-12; Proverbs 27:17; 1 Thessalonians 5:11; and Hebrews 10:24-25.

- What needs to change in men (including you) so that we can go deeper together?

- What does it mean to you, to "yield" to the Lordship and leadership of God in your life?

Week 2, Day 3

God's Man of Steel Does What is Right, Even When the Odds Are Stacked Against Him

"These are the names of the mighty men whom David had: Josheb-Basshebeth a Tahchemonite; he was chief of the three. He wielded his spear against eight hundred whom he killed at one time" (2 Samuel 23:8). Wait a minute … did you catch that? This guy killed 800 men at one time! Now that's a man of steel!

Josheb-Basshebeth was a Tahchemonite. We're talking William Wallace, Maximus Desimus Meridius and John Rambo all wrapped up into one. Dude, you don't want to mess with this guy! In this part of the story, Josheb finds himself in a rather tight situation, facing impossible odds. He's surrounded by 800 men who want him dead. 800 to 1. The likelihood of survival, let alone victory, doesn't look very good for poor Josheb.

Our hero is faced with a critical decision. A terrifying, life-changing decision. *"Do I turn tail and run like crazy, or do I stand my ground and fight?"* Okay, guys, I gotta ask—what would you do? I mean, really? Who in their right mind would choose to stick around in the face of those odds? Apparently, Josheb.

> ## Ephesians 6:10, 13
>
> *"Finally, be strong in the Lord and in the strength of his might. Therefore take up the whole armor of God, that you may be able to withstand in the evil day, and having done all, to stand firm."*

Don't forget that those 800 men weren't wimps. They weren't pansies. Josheb wasn't facing a bunch of green-behind-the-ears farmers armed with pitchforks (if you're a farmer, I mean no offense—unless you start charging at me with a pitchfork, that is). These were seasoned warriors with sharpened blades in hand. They had multiple notches in their belts, if you know what I mean.

These 800 blood-thirsty warriors had one specific target: Josheb. They had one specific goal: Josheb's death. So by all accounts, Josheb should have been easy pickings. And yet the Bible says he wielded his spear against all 800 and slaughtered every one of them.

Imagine for a moment that you are Philistine warrior #562. I wonder what would have been going through your mind as you stood there, watching your comrades dropping like flies at the might of this Tahchemonite. Suddenly he sets his eyes on you and comes charging. I can't answer for you, but I'm fairly positive I'd be dropping my sword, holding my hands up in front of me shouting, "Whoa, whoa—seriously—wait a minute! How are you doing this? Dude, who are you?"

I can just see the huge smile on Josheb's face as he pounds his chest and says, "I'm Josheb-Basshebeth, the Tahchemonite. Commander of the armies of the North. General of the fearless legions. Loyal servant to the true King. Father of a murdered son, husband of a murdered wife. And I will have my revenge, if not in this life, then in the next!" Well, I'm fairly certain he didn't actually say those exact words since that came from the movie *Gladiator*,[15] but you get my drift.

Have you ever been there? Have you ever been in a spot where you knew the odds were stacked against you? You knew there was no way you could win. You knew if you stood up for what was right, if you chose fight instead of flight, you risked losing everything. And yet, in spite of all of that, you stood for what you knew to be right no matter the cost. That, gentlemen—that is a man of steel. That is what makes a Super Man of God!

- I'm talking about the business owner who stands up and says, "No! I will not compromise God's standards just so I can get this sale or save a few extra bucks."
- I'm talking about the employee who sees what's going on behind the scenes and under the table, and refuses to be a part of it—even if it means his job.
- I'm talking about the teenager who refuses to do what everybody else is doing when he knows it's wrong, even though he's experiencing a relentless barrage of constant teasing and taunting of his peers.
- I'm also talking about the guy who says "No!" then turns and walks the other way when tempted to lust and commit adultery.

This is a mindset that says, *"No Retreat!"*

Remember, Josheb was not some superman from another planet. He wasn't gifted with the Force. He wasn't wearing a precious golden ring that gave him special abilities. He was just a normal, ordinary, everyday guy who was fully yielded to the Lordship and leadership of the Almighty, all-powerful God of the Universe.

Josheb chose to stand his ground in the face of certain defeat, and shout out to the enemy, "You shall not pass!" Then he fought with every fiber of his being until the task was accomplished. Josheb knew what you and I need to know: with God on our side, we have nothing and no one to fear!

God says, "I am the Lord, your God who takes hold of your right hand and says to you, 'Do not fear; I will help you'" (Isaiah 41:13). The only way you will overcome, the only way you will know victory when defeat feels certain, the only way you will effectively say "No!" to temptation when it comes knocking on your heart's door—the only way you can consistently be God's Man of Steel—is to completely yield yourself to the Lordship and leadership of the Almighty, all-powerful God of the Universe in your life. Not sometime this week. Not tomorrow. Not even in a few hours. Now. Right here, right now.

Give it Some Thought

- Why do you think Josheb chose to stand and fight, as opposed to running away?

- We face a foe far greater than 800 Philistine warriors (Ephesians 6:12). Read Ephesians 4:27. What are some ways we give the enemy a foothold?

- What is God's promise in James 4:7, and what two things are you to do?

- What does it mean to submit to God, and what does that look like? Write your answer below, then discuss as a group.

- How is a Super Man of God supposed to resist the Devil? Write your answer below, then discuss as a group.

- According to Ephesians 6:11, what are you supposed to do? (Note: the answer isn't only putting on the armor.)

Week 2, Day 4

God's Man of Steel Doesn't Give Up – Even When No One Stands With Him

Let me introduce you to Eleazar the Ahohite. Now this guy is the epitome of a normal, ordinary, everyday guy. He was discontented with life—nothing seemed to bring him happiness. So he tried various get-rich-quick schemes that got him in debt up to his eyeballs. Bottom line: he was in emotional and psychological distress as a result of some really bad choices.

Looking for a way out, he heard a rumor about a group of guys who were heading up to Adulam to pledge their loyalty to the one and only David-the-Giant-Slayer. Now there was a guy with promise. There was a guy who was going places. There was a guy Eleazar definitely wanted to meet.

Upon his arrival at David's camp, Eleazar was led to the mouth of a cave and told simply to wait. Looking around, he was shocked at what he saw—or rather, at what he didn't see. There were no royal banners flying high. There were no servants bustling about. In fact, there really wasn't much of anything very impressive. Just a few guys sitting on rocks looking bored or scared—or both.

After a few moments, this short, young scrawny-looking kid strode out of the cave. With a big smile on his face, he introduced himself as David. Eleazar was surprised—definitely not what he was expecting. Could this really be the famous Giant-Slayer he had heard so much about? He was so small and so, well, so skinny.

After a quick tour of the camp and a lengthy explanation as to why David was there, Eleazar decided he would like to join that motley crew. The accommodations weren't all that great. Living in a cave certainly had its perks, though—your creditors couldn't find you, and you certainly didn't have to worry much about housekeeping. But the dank surroundings, along with the stench of a bunch of guys camping out who hadn't bathed in weeks, certainly had their drawbacks.

A week or so later, as the sun was just beginning to rise in the east, a scout came running into the cave with the report of a legion of Philistine soldiers camping out on the other side of a large field a short distance away. David decided it was worth checking out, so he and his group of misfits grabbed their swords and headed out.

> ## Galatians 5:13
> *"For you were called to freedom, brothers. Only do not use your freedom as an opportunity for the flesh, but through love serve one another."*

Eleazar stood to David's left as they gathered at the opposite end of the field, cautiously surveying the Philistine encampment. The smoke rising from the enemy's campfires sat heavy on the countryside. Through the early morning haze, he could see distorted shapes of soldiers walking about. The sounds of their swords clanking and their guttural laughs left Eleazar with a solid weight rapidly growing at the bottom of his gut.

Suddenly David cupped his hands to his mouth, took a deep breath, and began to taunt and tease the Philistines. Eleazar watched as, one by one, his friends and cohorts followed David's lead. He couldn't believe what he was seeing. Seriously? Were they actually standing here yelling at the Philistines like a bunch of schoolyard kids? *"C'mon guys,"* Eleazar thought. *"What are you doing? What do you think is going to happen when you start poking at a hornet's nest?"*

Sure enough, as if on cue, the Philistine soldiers came pouring out of their tents, charging across the field toward David and his group of misfit warriors. Eleazar watched them come. He saw the bloodlust in their eyes. His own blood turned cold at the sound of their screams for revenge. Before he even knew what was happening, his sword was in his hand. "Alright, David, let's take these guys—we can do this!" he shouted. No response. "David?" Looking side to side, neither David nor his other friends were anywhere to be seen. Hearing a sound behind him he spun on his heel, ready to defend himself, only to see the shrinking backsides of his friends as they hightailed it out of there.

Stunned, he looked at the onslaught of warriors coming at him and then back at his friends. Eleazar was faced with a terrifying, life-changing decision. *"Do I live to fight another day, or is today a good day to die?"* Shrugging his shoulders, he turned to face the enemy. Planting his feet firmly in place, Eleazar raised his sword high and shouted, "Bring it! Because you shall not pass!"

Samuel says that "the men of Israel retreated, but (Eleazar) stood his ground and struck down the Philistines till his hand grew tired and froze to the sword. The Lord brought about a great victory that day" (2 Samuel 23:9-10). One man, one decision, one God, one amazing victory.

Guys, the ability to defeat the enemy was not within Eleazar. He could never have struck down every Philistine on that field of battle on his own. The only reason he could defeat the enemy, the only reason he was able to come away from that encounter in absolute victory, the only reason Eleazar was God's Man of Steel that day, was because he had fully yielded himself to the Lordship and leadership of the Almighty, all-powerful God of the Universe in his life. As a result, he became a tool in God's hand. No, it wasn't Eleazar who won that victory; it was the Lord![16]

> # Romans 8:37
> *"No, in all these things we are more than conquerors through him who loved us."*

Any time you try to fight the enemy in your own power, *you will fail!* It is only with God that we will gain the victory. Why? Because only He can trample our enemies![17]

God was with Eleazar when he faced down those Philistines all by himself. Yes, God gave Eleazar the victory. But Eleazar had to fight alone. He had to fight long, and he had to fight hard. In fact, he fought so long and so hard that he got the mother of all muscle cramps. His hand literally froze to the sword.

When the battle was over, after he had dispatched the last Philistine soldier, Eleazar dropped to his knees. Exhausted, covered in sweat and blood, he tipped his head back and screamed in sheer agony as he slowly pried his fingers off the hilt of his sword. As Eleazar fought, he gave it his all. That, my friend, is a man of steel. That is a mighty man of God.

Not only does God's man of steel have a mindset that says, *"No retreat,"* he also says, *"No reserve! I will hold nothing back. I will give everything I am and everything I have for my king."*

How about it, guys: Are you ready to give everything you are and everything you have for your King? Yes, you may be asked to stand on the battlefield alone. You may be required to fight the fight of faith with no one standing by your side. But do you understand that when you surrender to the Lordship and leadership of God in your life you are guaranteed the victory? The Almighty, all-powerful God of the Universe is within you. Truly, you can do all things through Christ because He will give you His strength! [18]

Give it Some Thought

- Write your answer below, then discuss as a group this question: Why do we tend to choose to "live to fight another day," as opposed to, "today is a good day to die"?

- Write your answer below, then discuss as a group how to apply the following verses: Romans 8:28, 31; Isaiah 8:9-10; 41:10; Psalm 118:6-9; and Jeremiah 20:11.

Week 2, Day 5

God's Man of Steel Stands in The Gap

In the movie trilogy entitled *The Lord of the Rings*, the first of the three feature films (*The Fellowship of the Ring*[19]) has a fantastically dramatic scene where the wizard Gandalf and his crew (including a dwarf, an elf, two humans and four Hobbits) are being chased through the mines of Moria by a fiery beast known as Balrog.

Running through the bowels of the mountain, they come upon a deep and dangerous chasm. Hard on their heels, Balrog comes charging at them, confident he has them cornered. Gandalf sees a narrow, fragile stone bridge that crosses the gap and urges the party to go on ahead of him to the other side. Once the last member of the group is safely over, Gandalf runs halfway across the bridge, stops, and turns to face the beast—intentionally placing himself between Balrog and his friends.

All alone on that bridge, Gandalf makes a difficult decision. He chooses to stand in the gap before the enemy. He makes the decision to take the full brunt of the beast's wrath so his friends don't have to. As he stands there facing Balrog, the most powerful scene in the entire movie begins to unfold. Looking the beast square in the eye, Gandalf raises his staff in one hand and his sword in the other, then shouts out in clear, unmistakable words, "You shall not pass!"

Today, as we close out the week, we are going to meet one more man from David's band of misfits—another of God's men of steel. His name is Shammah, yet another guy who was out of sorts. He had made some bad decisions in life and was definitely paying the consequences. I don't know if he just wasn't thinking, wasn't considering the cost, or what (if anything) was going on in his mind, but Shammah was in trouble. So, he headed for the hills and joined forces with David. Little did he know what God was planning to do in his life.

You see, an army of Philistines had gathered at the fields of Lehi, intent on destroying a huge crop of beans. They knew that if they could drive the Israelites to hunger, it would weaken their will and ability to fight. A very cunning strategy. Starve your enemy, then when they don't have enough strength to raise a finger (let alone a sword) to object, march right in and slaughter them. The only thing those Philistines didn't take into account was Shammah.

Once again the enemy charges forward. Once again David's crew of normal, ordinary, everyday guys turn tail and run. And as the dust settles, standing in the middle of the field, standing in the gap before the enemy, is Shammah. Sword drawn, a look of determination on his face, heart exploding in his chest, unsure of what was about to happen, he plants his feet and shouts to the enemy, "Bring it, because you shall not pass!"

Shammah wasn't anybody special. He didn't have any superpowers. He didn't have steel claws that shot out of his hands on command. He couldn't take over the minds of the Philistines and make them turn against each other. He couldn't even become invisible. And yet, as he took his stand in the middle of that field of beans, Shammah—a man fully yielded to the Lordship and leadership of the Almighty, all-powerful God of the Universe—struck down the Philistines. Every last one of them.[20]

God Wants YOU
Today God is looking for men of steel. He is looking for men who will build up the wall and stand in the gap. He is searching for men who will draw their swords, stand before the enemy and shout out at the top of their lungs, "You shall not pass!" God wants men of integrity, men of conviction, men of courage—men of steel. He wants you, my friend.

> ## Jeremiah 20:11
> *"But the Lord is with me like a mighty warrior; so my persecutors will stumble and not prevail. They will fail and be thoroughly disgraced; their dishonor will never be forgotten."*

"Oh, not me. Certainly, not me!" you say. Why not? Seriously. Why not you? *"Well, I just don't think I could do it. It's just not who I am."* May I remind you that Josheb, Eleazar and Shammah didn't think they could do it, either? They were just normal, ordinary, everyday guys.

Just like you. Just like me. Josheb wasn't Iron Man. Eleazar wasn't Thor, God of Thunder. Shammah wasn't The Incredible Hulk. Don't lose sight of the fact that these were just normal, ordinary guys who chose to fully yield themselves to the Lordship and leadership of the Almighty, all-powerful God of the Universe.

Guys, every one of us going through this study—no matter who you are, no matter what you've done, no matter where you are in your spiritual walk—every one of us is commanded to "be strong and courageous. Do not be frightened, and do not be dismayed, for the Lord your God is with you wherever you go" (Joshua 1:9).

If there ever was a time for us to be men of steel—if there ever was a time for us to be Super Men of God who stand up for the Gospel, who stand up for the Kingdom, who stand up for righteousness, who stand up for purity and for the glory of God—that time is now!

God is calling you out, right here and right now. No, I'm not talking about (or to) the other guy in your group. I'm not talking to the guy who should be reading this book. I'm talking to you—yes, you. God is calling *you* to rise up against the darkness of this world. He is calling *you* to draw your sword, stand firm in the faith and fight for His kingdom. Fight with everything you have and everything you are. Will you take that stand? Be a Super Man and shout to the enemy, in the name of Christ, "Bring it, because you shall not pass!"

Give it Some Thought
- Share with the guys at least one takeaway you received from this week, and what you plan to do about it.

"Therefore, everyone who hears these words of mine and puts them into practice is like a wise man who built his house on the rock."
Matthew 7:24 NIV '84

Week 3
A Super House for a Super Man

Week 3, Day 1

It's a fact: superheroes can't fight crime and save lives around the clock. Sometimes they just need a place to get away from it all. A place to relax. A place to recharge. For Superman, that place is called "The Secret Citadel" (a.k.a. The Fortress of Solitude).[1]

Located somewhere way up north in the frozen tundra of the Arctic stands the Fortress of Solitude. It's a place known only to Superman, a place only he can get to. It's that one place Superman goes when he needs to be alone with his thoughts. It's that one place where he can truly experience safety, security, and a connection to his real home—Krypton. A super house for a super man.

The Fortress offers Superman the opportunity to be himself, a Kryptonian, rather than Clark Kent of the Daily Planet. It is the one place in the entire universe that reminds him of who he really is, and what he stands for—truth, justice and the American way.

The Fortress is also the one place where Superman can go to talk with his father, Jor-El. Through a special device called the Crystal of Knowledge, Jor-El communicates with his son and offers him counsel and guidance in how to deal with the problems that arise from living on an alien world. It's a relationship that Kal-El (Superman) cherishes deeply.

My Fortress of Solitude

- Read Philippians 3:20. As a child of God, where are you from —where is "home"?

- While here on earth, what does that make you (see 1 Peter 2:11)?

As a Super Man of God, you too need a place to relax and recharge. You need a place where you can experience safety, security and a connection to your real home. You need a Fortress of Solitude. Guys, it's vitally important that we never lose sight of the fact that this world is not our home.[2] We are strangers and aliens in a foreign land—a land that is not and cannot ever be our friend. This world is against the things of God. It is against holiness. It is against godliness. It is against righteousness and purity. Because you are a Christian man, it is against you.[3]

Did you know there is a perfect place God created just for you here on earth? A Spiritual Fortress of Solitude. A Secret Citadel. A Holy Refuge. A place of communion and fellowship with your Father. It's the one place in the entire universe that will remind you of who you really are (a child of the King) and what you really stand for (godliness, righteousness and the way of godliness).

In Psalm 46 we read a powerful description of our mighty fortress.

> "God is our refuge and strength, an ever-present help in trouble. Therefore we will not fear, though the earth give way and the mountains fall into the heart of the sea, though its waters roar and foam and the mountains quake with their surging. *Selah* ... The Lord Almighty is with us;

the God of Jacob is our fortress … 'Be still and know that I am God; I will be exalted among the nations, I will be exalted in the earth.' The Lord Almighty is with us; the God of Jacob is our fortress. *Selah.*" (Psalm 46:1-3, 7, 10-11)

Run to that fortress, my friend, run to God; for it is there, in a growing, vibrant, powerful relationship with God, that you will find joy, peace and safety.

In that fortress you also have a "Crystal of Knowledge" (your Bible), through which your Heavenly Father communicates with you and offers you wise counsel and guidance in how to deal with the problems that arise from living in an alien, sinful world. But are you using it? Are you daily linking to it so you can connect with the Father? Are you dropping to your knees in prayer, communicating with your Divine Dad, and poring over Scripture, listening to what He's telling you?

This week we are going to look at the kind of house you are building. What materials are you putting into your spiritual home, and how is it standing up in the storms of life? Is it a fortress of solitude or a teetering tower of twigs ready to fall over at the slightest breath of the big bad wolf who is crouching at your door?[4]

Building on a Solid Foundation

Pause for a moment and think about the house (or apartment) where you currently live. If you were asked to describe it, what would you say? You might decide to talk about its location, the size of the lot it sits on and the kind of neighborhood it's in. More than likely you'd mention the number of bedrooms and bathrooms it has; possibly even its color, design, and square footage. But you probably wouldn't talk about its foundation. Truth be told, the likelihood of it even crossing your mind is slim to none. Yet it is the foundation of your home that makes all the difference in the world.

When a home is being built, it's wise to start with a foundation. That only makes sense, right? After all, what happens to the structure if you build upon a weak foundation, or choose not to have one at all? Do you remember the children's story of the Three Little Pigs? Two of them chose to build their homes out of straw and sticks. Oh, they were wonderful to look at (if you're a pig, that is). They even remained standing for a brief period of time. However, as soon as a strong wind came along—WHAM! Down they went.

Which kind of home would you want to live in: one built on a weak foundation or one built on a strong one? Seems like a silly question. After all, what sane person would want to live in a house built on a poor foundation (that is, unless you're a little pig thinking you're safe from the big bad wolf)? Just as a solid foundation is needed in order to build a solid structure, so we need to build our spiritual lives on a spiritually solid foundation.

The truth is, life can be hard. If you expect to stay standing in the midst of the storms of life that constantly bombard you on every front, you need to be planted firmly on a foundation that will not fail—one that runs deep into solid rock.

Let's dream for a moment. What would it be like to live the rest of your life built on a foundation that will never shake, rattle or roll? Wouldn't you love to live your life secure in the knowledge that absolutely no storm, no matter how intense, could ever destroy you? I know I can't put words in your mouth, but I'm going to assume your answer is a loud and boisterous "Yes!" Am I right?

Gentlemen, I challenge you—don't ever lose sight of the fact that as a Christian man, the most important thing you could ever do is know God and live in a way that always brings honor and glory to Him.[5] In order to live that kind of life—even in the worst of storms—you must build that life into a solid, spiritual foundation; God's foundation.

Before ever going high, you must first go deep.

You see, when you build your life deep into God's foundation, that life is guaranteed to stand firm at all times.[6] That doesn't mean you won't have storms in life. (Wouldn't that be nice?) However, it does mean that when you build your life upon a growing relationship with God, those storms will never take you down—that is His promise.[7] That is a promise you can take to the bank of Heaven, the safest, most secure bank in the entire universe.[8]

The question, then, is this: What is the foundation we should build our godly lives upon, and how do we start building on it? The answer is both simple and complex. You see, *you* don't have to try to lay this foundation (insert big sigh of relief). The foundation has already been laid in the person of Jesus Christ.[9] The real question is, what are you doing this very moment to build your relationship with Christ?

There's an old hymn of the faith that is worth visiting here. Read these words and let their truth sink deep into your soul.

> "My hope is built on nothing less
> Than Jesus' blood and righteousness;
> I dare not trust the sweetest frame,
> But wholly lean on Jesus' name.
>
> Refrain:
> "On Christ, the solid Rock, I stand;
> All other ground is sinking sand,
> All other ground is sinking sand.
>
> "When darkness veils His lovely face,
> I rest on His unchanging grace;
> In every high and stormy gale,
> My anchor holds within the veil.
>
> "His oath, His covenant, His blood
> Support me in the whelming flood;
> When all around my soul gives way,
> He then is all my hope and stay.
>
> Refrain:
> "On Christ, the solid Rock, I stand;
> All other ground is sinking sand,
> All other ground is sinking sand."[10]

Give it Some Thought
- What is the purpose of a house? How do you feel knowing your house is built on a solid foundation? Why?

- Which kind of spiritual life do you want to live: one that is built on a weak foundation or one built on a strong one? Why?

- What are you doing *right now* to build your life on a strong, spiritually solid foundation?

- How do we, as men, build godly lives?

- Why, as men, do we struggle with the concept of having a "relationship" with God?

Week 3, Day 2

During my grandfather's generation, when building a home, the very first stone laid in the foundation was always strategically placed in the corner of the structure (probably why they ingeniously called it the cornerstone). It was the most important part of the entire building. That one stone determined the position of all the stones to be laid afterward. In fact, the placement of that stone determined the setting of the entire structure. If the cornerstone wasn't placed just right, the entire building would be permanently off of true.

What is the cornerstone of your life? Is it the stone of pleasure? How about the stone of success or the stone of happiness? Maybe it's the stone of fortune or popularity. Whatever that stone may be, it is truly the most important stone in the structure called your life. It determines the direction your life is going to take. So carefully consider this next point: if you choose to build your life around any stone other than Christ, your structure (your life) will be "off"—guaranteed.

In Scripture Jesus is called the Chief Cornerstone.[11] King David wrote, "The Lord is the stronghold of my life—of whom shall I be afraid?" (Psalm 27:1). He also said, "The Lord is a refuge for the oppressed, a stronghold in times of trouble" (Psalm 9:9). David is saying that Jesus Christ is your place of safety and refuge in the times of trouble; He is your rock that will keep you secure. In fact, He IS the only foundation you will ever need. Build your life upon Him and you are guaranteed to stand no matter what storm tries to take you down. A growing relationship with Jesus Christ is your Fortress of Solitude!

Our Crystal of Knowledge

Did you know that the best way to discover who Jesus is and how to get to know Him is to open your Bible and study the pages of God's Word? In fact, take a moment right now and pick up your Bible—hold it in your hand and look at it. Open the pages and glance at the words.

- How do you feel about your Bible? (No, this is not a trick question, so answer honestly.)

Seriously, now, how do you truly feel about it? Is it just a book that sits on a shelf or on your coffee table during the week, only to be picked up and opened briefly on Sundays during the morning message? Is it a book you open each morning as you read the three verses your daily devotional guide requires while having a cup of coffee and bagel (or if you're like me, a glass of milk and chocolate chip cookies)? Or do you cry out with David, "Oh, how I love your law! I meditate on it all day long"? (Psalm 119:97). Is your delight "in the law of the Lord" and on that law do you "meditate day and night"? (Psalm 1:2).

Why is that so important? Why is it critical that I *love* my Bible? Isn't it enough that I occasionally read it? Take a few moments here and think about the amazing letter God has written *to you* called The Bible. In fact, as you read these next bullet points, pick up your Bible once again and hold it in your hand. I know, sounds a bit weird, but try it. Now consider this:

- God's Word is living, active, sharper than any double-edged sword. Every time you read it, study it, memorize it and meditate on it, Scripture pushes aside all the junk and fluff in life and gets right to the heart of the matter.[12]
- The Bible contains the very words of God. It is quite literally God speaking to you, teaching you deep and wonderful truths about Himself and Heaven and how He wants you to live. It rebukes us when we do wrong. It shows us how to make it right and trains us in how to live consistently godly lives.[13]
- It brings blessing to those who hear it and obey its commands.[14]
- Because God is true, God's Word is also true—there is no error in it,[15] and therefore it will never lead us down a wrong path.[16]
- It was written to provide us with godly instruction on how to live in a way that honors our Heavenly Father, providing us with great hope.[17]
- It helps us become spiritually prosperous and genuinely successful.[18]
- It always draws us to God and it is reliable, trustworthy and full of wisdom; when we read it and obey its commands, it brings great joy to our souls and will never lead us astray.[19]
- It helps us grow in our walk with God.[20]
- It stands forever and will never pass away.[21]
- It is to be kept diligently,[22] it will help us keep our way pure,[23] it teaches us good judgment,[24] it makes us wiser than our enemies,[25] gives us more understanding than the smartest teacher or the elderly,[26] and guides our every step in life.[27]

That's just a partial list! We could take up this entire study with statements on the value of Scripture and the joys of growing in our relationship with God. We have been given a sure and solid foundation! This is what we must build a godly life upon if we expect to stand firm in the storms of life.

Give it Some Thought
- When you hear the words "Jesus is our Cornerstone," what does that mean to you?

- Is He your Cornerstone? How do we make Him our Cornerstone?

- How has your study of the Bible impacted your life? Write your answer below, then discuss as a group.

Week 3, Day 3

Are You a Wise Man or a Moron?
How's that for an opening question? Does it intrigue you or offend you? Jesus sure had a way of doing that to people. You see, He asked that very question in Matthew 7.

In Matthew 7 Jesus introduces us to Wally and Martin (names I made up for the sake of this study). Wally is a wise man, and Martin is a moron. Oh, that's not my description of Martin, it's Christ's.

Now, I'm willing to bet if you pick up your Bible and read Matthew 7:24-27, you will not find the word "moron." But I assure you—it's there. Jesus called Martin a "foolish" man. That word comes from the Greek word "*moros.*" You guessed it, it's the same as our English word moron. And it means exactly what you would expect the word to mean—one who is stupid, a blockhead, a very foolish man.

So, who are these two guys? What are they building? What makes Wally wise and Martin a moron? Enquiring minds want to know!

Let the Construction Begin
The first thing we need to focus on is the magnitude of their building project. They weren't assembling a really cool treehouse or an ice-fishing shanty or duck blind. They were building a very important structure which Jesus called their "house." In other words, both of these guys were deeply involved in their life-building project.

This wasn't a fly-by-night, do it on a whim and slap it together kind of thing. This was an I'm-all-in, do-or-die project. Their goal wasn't simply to construct a comfy vacation bungalow somewhere in the Hamptons. They weren't building something just for themselves. It was to be a heritage for their kids—a legacy they hoped would last well into the future. They were building their lives.

In a few moments, we will discover together just what made Martin a moron and Wally wise. But for right now keep in mind that Martin wasn't just throwing a few sticks together with spit, chewing gum and a ball of twine and saying—voilà, there is my life! He wasn't going through the building process thinking, *"Oh, this is just a temporary thing. I know a big bad wolf is going to come along someday and he'll huff and he'll puff, and when he blows, everything I've worked for all my life will come crashing down around me."* He didn't shrug his shoulders and say, *"Eh, no big deal. When it does collapse, I'll just pick up the pieces of my life and start all over again."* No! He was just as intent on building a life that would leave a lasting legacy as was his counterpart. Both he and Wally were working toward the same goal.

You and I strongly resemble the builders of Matthew 7. Every day, whether we realize it or not, we are building into our lives as well. Every day, we make decisions that impact our lives and affect those around us. Every choice we make today determines the path we are going to go down tomorrow, and the heritage we will leave behind when we are gone.

Most of the time we don't pause long enough to consider that the things we choose to do (or not do) today are literally molding our future and setting a course that will influence the lives of everyone we care about. Not only do Wally and Martin share this similarity, but we have at least this one thing in common with both of them. We are all life-builders.

It's a Beautiful Day in the Neighborhood – or Is It?
The second similarity Wally and Martin shared is this: they both lived in the same neighborhood and probably knew each other. I say that because Jesus said they both encountered the exact same horrific storm that attacked their houses (lives). Christ said, "The rain came down, the streams rose, and the winds blew and beat against that house" (Matthew 7:25, 27).

This was no mild mid-summer thunderstorm. They didn't sit out on the back deck with an iced tea in hand and watch the clouds darken while complaining about their lumbago. The storm that ransacked their neighborhood was more like a class-five hurricane with a couple of tornadoes thrown in. That particular storm packed such a punch that it put untold stress on both of their lives. It bore down on both of them with unbearable force and they were powerless to do anything about it.

> ## Proverbs 3:5-6
> *"Trust in the Lord with all your heart and lean not on your own understanding; in all your ways acknowledge him, and he will make your paths straight."*

You and I will also face multiple storms in life—each one intent on destroying us. Sometimes we will get rained on. I'm not talking about droplets of moisture that fall from the sky—I'm referring to those tiny little situations (dare I say annoyances?) that in and of themselves don't amount to much, just a pesky drop here and there that we could definitely do without, but can tolerate. However, when they start hitting you all at once you find yourself diving for cover. Every so often the rain will fall on your life with a vengeance; how will you hold up under the barrage? The choices and decisions you make today will determine your answer when the storm comes tomorrow.

Sometimes, with the rain comes the flood. I'm talking about those situations in life that seem to swell up on you suddenly and then tend to just sit there, weighing heavily on you, drowning out everything you value. They just take over. You wonder if it will ever end, when it will go away. You feel a damp sadness creep over you, bordering on cold despair as it leaves sludge and destruction in its wake. The floods of life will come, my friend; you can count on it. The choices and decisions you make today will determine how you respond when it rises up all around you tomorrow.

And then there is the wind. This isn't a slight breeze we're talking about. I'm referring to the times when you get slammed, seemingly out of nowhere. You never saw it coming. This is the major surprise that hits you hard, relentlessly pressing in on you. You stagger back from the blast, barely able to keep your footing. You search for something (or someone) solid to grab hold of because you are unable to anchor yourself. You know if you don't find purchase soon, it's going to blow you far, far away. I'm sure you know what I'm talking about because you've experienced these winds before. And you will experience them again. The choices and decisions you make today will determine how solidly you stand against the wind tomorrow.

The fact is, life isn't always sunshine. It doesn't matter who you are or where you are spiritually, the storms will come. In fact, many times you'll get hit by rain *and* flooding *and* winds all at the same time.

How well will your structure (your life) hold up under the storm that's coming? What high-quality materials are you building into your life right now that will enable it to stand when the attack comes?

We don't know when the next storm is going to hit, how hard it will hit, how long it will last, or what part of our life it's going to attack. The only thing we do know is that it *will* come. We need to prepare now for the inevitable. So far, we share at least two things in common with Wally and Martin.

Give it Some Thought
- We saw that both builders faced the same storm. What storms of life have you struggled against? Why did you consider them "storms"?

- Read 1 Peter 5:8 and compare with John 8:44, 10:10. What does Satan want to accomplish through your storms, and why?

- Read James 1:2-3 and compare with Job 23:10; 1 Peter 1:7. What does God want to accomplish through your storms, and why?

Week 3, Day 4

It's Sunday-Go-To-Meetin' Time!
We've seen two similarities so far between Wally and Martin: first, each is building his life, his lasting legacy. Second, they are facing the same storm, intent on taking down both of their houses. A third connection these guys share is that they both attended the same church. They sat under the same pastor and were exposed to the same sermons week after week.

Please understand that in this story Jesus isn't saying that Wally had a love for hearing the Truth, while Martin felt utter contempt for it. No, Jesus said that both these guys *heard* the Word of God. Let me repeat that—they *both* heard God's Word! Sometimes we forget that part of the story. Both men knew the value of what God had to say. Both men sought it out. Both of these guys *listened* to what the Lord had to say.

> ## Ecclesiastes 5:1
> *"Guard your steps when you go to the house of God. To draw near to listen is better than to offer the sacrifice of fools, for they do not know that they are doing evil."*

Lest you think, *"Well, they may have heard the word of God, but only Wally was really listening,"* let me clarify something. The verb "to hear," as used in this story of the two builders in Matthew 7, indicates that the one doing the hearing is considering every word carefully. In other words, both Wally and Martin gave their full attention to what was being said, and they were thinking about how God's Truth applied to them.

Let me risk a moment of repetition here: don't lose sight of the fact that both of these builders *heard* God's Word. Both of them sat on the edge of the pew during the Sunday message. Both of them took notes and gave careful attention to what God had to say about how to live life, and gave serious thought to how it applied to them.

This wasn't just a wise-man thing to do. Even the other guy across the aisle sat there listening to what God had to say and was actually thinking about what he was hearing. Martin wasn't a moron—at least not yet.

Have you ever stopped to consider the fact that you too hear God's Word? You've been hearing it as you work your way through this study. You hear it every Sunday in church, or when you have your devotions or sit in a small group Bible study. Every time you hear God's Word you have a choice. What are you going to do with what you hear? Think about this carefully, because this is a third thing you and I share in common with Wally and Martin.

As thought-provoking as all of this is, it's not the similarities between these two guys (and us) that are important here. Up to this point, there is very little difference between the two men. However, Jesus makes it clear that there is just one single difference we need to focus our attention on. That sole variation is what determines whether you are a wise man or a moron. You see, the fundamental difference between Wally and Martin was the foundation they chose to build upon. Wally chose obedience to God's Word. Martin did not.

The foolish man of Matthew 7 heard God's Word, just like the wise man. What made him a moron was that he willfully chose to ignore what God had said. He heard God's truth, just as you are. He understood God's promises, just as you do. Yet he didn't follow through with obedience. (How about you?) Maybe he intended to apply God's principles to his life later on; I don't know. But James warns us to "not merely listen to the word, and so deceive yourselves. Do what it says" (James 1:22). Otherwise, you're a moron.

Martin made the choice to go about his life on his own. For whatever reason, he decided he only needed God on Sundays and holidays. What choices are you making *right now*? Think about this: you've already been spending time at the construction site. You are already fully engaged in your life-building project. The question, then, is not whether you are *going to be* a wise builder; rather, the real question is which builder are you right now? I can't repeat this enough. You are building your life right now. Is it a godly life? This very moment as you are reading these very words, would God consider you a wise man or a moron?

If you are not in God's Word daily, and if you are not applying God's truth to your life—moment-by-moment living in obedience to what God is teaching you—then I submit that you already are that foolish man. You are a moron. I know that's strong language, but if you truly want to be godly in your everyday living, it begins now. Not tomorrow, not after you're done going through this study, but now!

Let me reiterate the fact that God says a wise man will give his full and immediate attention to what God is saying in His Word. The wise man, the Super Man of God, is always considering carefully what he is reading, and he is seeking to understand how it applies to him. But that alone doesn't make us wise. Something else is required.

According to Jesus, it is nothing short of complete obedience! You have to put what God says into practice in your life.

Give it Some Thought

- Read James 1:22-23; 3 John 11; Luke 6:46; and Colossians 3:17. Most Christians "hear" God's Word. What does it mean to put it into practice?

- How does one put God's Word into "practice"? (Note: this is referring to more than just compliance to a set of rules.)

- Read Psalm 33:4, 119:105, 130; 2 Timothy 3:16-17; and Luke 11:28. Why is obeying God's Word a requirement for being a wise builder?

Week 3, Day 5

Practice Makes Perfect – Right?

During his elementary school years, our second child decided he wanted to learn how to play the violin. As many parents do, we jumped on board with the idea, bought him a violin and paid for private lessons. I would take him to his lesson, drop him off for an hour and then pick him up when the lesson was over. He would then stand in our living room and practice his music. It's amazing how great a child's playing can sound when filtered through strategically placed cotton balls!

One time I decided to sit in on his lesson, just to see how things were going. His teacher was a very patient and understanding woman, but I could see she was frustrated with him. I learned that day that the proper way to stroke the bow across the strings is primarily with your shoulder firmly fixed, using your elbow as the pivotal point. My boy was doing just the opposite—keeping the elbow firmly set, he would rock the bow with his shoulder.

Standing behind him, this woman—whom I've since nominated for sainthood—patiently squeezed his shoulder, forcing him to use his elbow. I'll never forget her stopping my son in mid-stroke and asking him, "Practice makes what?" Smiling, my boy responded with what he thought was the correct answer. "Perfect!" he exclaimed. "No!" she retorted. "Practice does NOT make perfect. Practice makes permanent —so you must practice right!" I'm not sure my son learned that valuable lesson (at least as it related to playing the violin), but it definitely had a profound impact upon me.

To be a wise man, to be a Super Man of God, you must not only hear what God is saying, but also seek to understand how it applies to you. Then, as the Holy Spirit guides you,[28] make the necessary adjustments to your daily behavior so you can consistently live out God's truth and principles. When you do this, God says you are a wise builder. This is when your godly life will be established upon a solid foundation. Remember, practice makes permanent—so practice right.

- How do Luke 11:28, John 14:15, 23 and 2 John 1:6 apply here?

What made Wally wise was hearing God's Word and choosing to put it into practice immediately. Wally didn't wait to obey until he felt like it, he didn't hold off until it fit into his schedule or plan. He didn't pick and choose which passages of Scripture he liked and do only them. He acted upon what God said to him at that very moment, every moment of his life.

I find it interesting that Wally didn't simply *set* his house on that rock, he dug deep into it![29] Obedience demands action; it requires effort; it calls for discipline. And sometimes it includes spiritual sweat. Wally couldn't rent a 385 CAT Excavator to dig into the rock. He didn't have access to a pneumatic jackhammer with alloy steel forgings and a four-bolt backhead design. In fact, he couldn't even find a simple stick of dynamite. All he had was a chisel, a hammer, and sheer brute force.

It takes work to build into the Rock. It requires time and energy, and it costs more. Let's face it, it's always easier to take shortcuts in building a home. You save money when you use inferior materials. And for a while, no one may notice the shoddy work. But somewhere along the line, there is a price to be paid.

It also takes less time and energy to maintain a superficial faith. To be honest, who will be able to tell the difference? It's definitely easier to just show up for church for an hour a week, let the worship leader and the pastor fill you with warm fuzzies, smile and shake hands as you go on your merry did-my-spiritual-duty-for-the-week way. It's less demanding on your day to just open the daily devotional booklet, read the few verses there, read the writer's comments, close it up, and go on with your day feeling content with your "God time."

The question for you is: Are you *doing* the Word? Are you, moment-by-moment, day-by-day choosing to do what God says? If you construct your life according to Christ's building codes, and if you dig deep into solid rock, you will not be disappointed.[30]

Give it Some Thought
- What is the difference between spending and investing?

- Do you tend to spend time or invest time in God's Word?

- In what ways can investing time in God's Word make a difference?

- Read James 1:22. What are you doing *today* to build a godly life? If your honest answer is "not much," what specific steps are you going to take to be that wise builder?

- Share with the guys at least one takeaway you received this week, and what you plan to do about it.

"For though by this time you ought to be teachers, you need someone to teach you again the basic principles of the oracles of God. You need milk, not solid food, for everyone who lives on milk is unskilled in the word of righteousness, since he is a child."
Hebrews 5:12-13

Week 4
A Super Meal for a Super Man

Week 4, Day 1

Breakfast for Champions

To live daily as a Super Man of God, it is critical that you always follow a specific spiritual "diet." It's vital that you are daily feeding upon God's Word. I'm not talking about Spiritual Melba Toast and a bowl of Holy Corn Flakes doused with a quarter-cup of Milk of the Word, here. I'm not referring to that short little thing many of us do in the morning that we tend to call "devotions." I'm talking about a thick, juicy, godly T-bone, medium-well, seasoned just right with a side of piping hot steak fries and a pile of scrambled eggs! I'm talking about a sit-down with your Bible, notepad next to you and pen in hand, with a sheer determination not to get up until you have discovered buried treasure, kind of meal. A man's meal. A Super Man's meal. How often do you eat like that? How often do you genuinely "feed" upon God's Word?

- Write your answer here:

The Old Testament prophet Jeremiah couldn't get enough of his Bible. In fact, he likened his reading of God's Word to eating a full course meal—drawing all the nourishment and strength he needed to live a godly life directly from the pages of Scripture.[5] Peter instructs us to deeply desire the Word of God, because it's Scripture that helps us grow up in our relationship with our Heavenly Father.[6] To be a Super Man of God, you gotta eat right, eat often and eat well.

Have you ever noticed that you rarely see Super Man eat? Ever wonder why that is? Since eating is all about providing energy to the body, and since Superman's physiology draws all his energy from the sun, he really has no reason or need to eat. But I'm willing to bet that he dines on occasion just so he can enjoy the company of a certain female reporter for the Daily Planet named Lois Lane.

How about you? No, I'm not asking if you want to go out on a date with Lois Lane. Nor am I talking about your appetite for spaghetti and meatballs. Actually, I'm more interested in this: as a Super Man of God, do you eat? What do you eat? What kind of spiritual food are you feeding upon? How often do you eat? Do you even *need* to eat?

Don't Just Sit There – Eat Already!
I know of some people who, when sitting at a table in a restaurant, study the menu from cover to cover. Ever meet someone like that? You sit down, glance at the menu that was handed you, find what you want and you're ready to order. Then there are those who read through every item, twice. They examine it, evaluate it, even discuss it with everyone else at the table. But when the wait staff comes to take your order, they ask for a few more minutes. Frustrating, right?

All too often, as Christian men, that's how we treat the Word of God. We see it as a menu to be examined, evaluated and discussed rather than a full-course meal to be consumed and enjoyed. As a result, many men are suffering from a sort of spiritual anorexia. Instead of feeding upon the banquet of blessing that God has prepared in His Word, they are starving themselves.

Feeding your physical body is good; hey, sometimes it can be very good (I myself am a huge fan of liver and onions—now there's a dish fit for a king)! But "man shall not live by bread alone, but by every word that comes from the mouth of God" (Matthew 4:4).

As a Super Man of God, I must draw my strength, I must find my sustenance, from God's Word. Without it, I become weak and vulnerable. In Week 3, Day 2 I asked you to answer the question,

"How do you feel about your Bible?" You may have chosen not to write out your answer, and I get that. But even if you didn't write it out, you have already answered it. You answer that question every day of your life. How? By your actions. The things you say, the choices you make, the actions you take reflect your view of God's Word.

- Read Psalm 1:1-3. According to verse two, what word describes how the guy feels who is in God's Word day and night?

- According to verse one, because he delights in God's Word, what are his choices and actions like?

- According to verse three, what's the result of delighting in God's Word?

Guys, please note the fact that God doesn't say that the man who *appreciates* His Word, or the man who *respects* His Word will be like a tree, yielding fruit and prospering. He doesn't say that the man who brings his Bible to church and does daily devotions is the one who will be blessed. It's the guy who delights in God's Word and meditates on it daily. Are you that guy? Do you want to be?

Give it Some Thought

- Read the Psalm 119:25-32. What are all the references to God's Word in this text? (e.g. "statutes"—look hard; there are at least 8 depending on the translation you are reading)

- Just like you need physical food for physical strength, you need spiritual food for spiritual strength. The Bible describes itself as our spiritual food—it's the water, milk, bread, and meat of our spiritual lives. It's everything we need for sustenance. What does feeding on God's Word look like?

- From Psalm 119:25-32, what is the result of being in God's Word? (Hint: there are at least 6.)

Week 4, Day 2

Delighting 101

Warning: I'm gonna get sappy for a moment—but hey, I'm the author, I can do that.

I remember back in college when my wife and I were dating. As I got to know her, I found myself constantly thinking about her. Every moment we were apart was sheer agony. I couldn't wait until class was over and I could be with her again.

> ## Psalm 1:1-2
> *"Blessed is the man who walks not in the counsel of the wicked, nor stands in the way of sinners, nor sits in the seat of scoffers; but his delight is in the law of the Lord, and on his law he meditates day and night."*

The long walks we took as the sun set were pure heaven. I hung on her every word (her thick Bostonian accent didn't hurt either). The more I learned about her, the more I wanted to know; and the more time I invested with her, the more I wanted to be with her. I truly delighted in her—and still do. Today, over 36 years later, every moment we're apart my heart aches (there's the sappy part). It's true. I can't wait for the workday to be over so we can be together again.

I look forward to sitting at the dinner table and listening to her as she tells me about her day. I am so privileged, honored, and humbled to be able to say that I still delight in my wonderful wife!

The guy who "delights" in God's Word is the guy who finds great pleasure in reading it. He can't wait for the moment when he can open its pages and study it, just to hear God speak to him. He's the guy who sees the value in using it to address his problems; and he's anxious about living it out in his life. Do you feel that way about your Bible? Do you delight in God's Word?

Oh, but that flies in the face of everything we've been taught about being men! Delighting in God sure doesn't sound very manly. It doesn't growl like a 2.2-liter twin turbo V-6 putting out 700 hp. It doesn't pop and kick like a Kalashnikov AK-47 assault rifle. It's not like running 10 grueling miles through 500,000 gallons of Grade-A mud, 40 tons of ice and over 20 excruciating obstacles, all designed to wear you down and drag you out of your comfort zone. Now that's manhood! Right?

I agree that "delighting" in God and His Word doesn't sound very manly. But I challenge you—no, strike that—I DARE you to try it. Try delighting in God's Word while the world around you is screaming in your ear for attention. Just try focusing all of your heart, mind and soul on growing in your walk with God while the job is stressful, and the car is giving you fits, and the bills are mounting. Go ahead and see if you can go deeper in your relationship with God in spite of all the sexual lust that surrounds you on every street corner and with every click of the mouse. Ain't no two ways about it, delighting in God and His Word is tough! It takes a real man, a Super Man, to do that.

Do you want to be a Super Man of God? Find delight in God's Word. Do you want to be a man of integrity, a man who garners respect from those around him? You need to long for the time each day when you can sit down with your Bible and listen to your Father speak to you. Seriously, dude—no joke!

I like the way author and preacher Tony Evans put it: *"You know you are getting somewhere in your spiritual growth when you can feed yourself from God's Word, instead of having to have it all chopped up and prepared and spooned into your mouth. And when you can help feed someone else on the Word, you are showing the marks of a mature believer.*

"To develop spiritual maturity requires that you read God's Word so you know what it says (Revelation 1:3), study the Word so you know what it means (2 Timothy 2:15), memorize the Word so you can use it when you need it (Psalm 119:11), and take every opportunity to hear the Word of God proclaimed and taught so we can learn to live life and make decisions based on it (Hebrews 5:13-14)."[1]

A Super Man of God gives that kind of serious attention to his Bible. Guys, BE that Super Man!

Give it Some Thought
- Read the following verses and note what is said about the value of God's Word.
  - Psalm 119:72 – In your own words, what is God's Word better than?

- Joshua 1:8 – When does a man find prosperity and success?

- Psalm 119:92 – What is David really saying here?

- Read Job 23:12 and Jeremiah 15:16. Let's be real here. When there's so much value in God's Word, why do we struggle so much with investing time in it?

Week 4, Day 3

Eric stood as tall as he could while his dad knelt in front of him. He had been looking forward to this day all week long. Every day after school he would run downstairs to the basement, drag the chair over to dad's chin-up bar, tie the two-pound weights on his ankles, grab hold of the bar and hang there for two whole minutes!

"Mommy said that the doctor said that Sissy grew a whole half finch. I'll bet I've growed at least a foot, Daddy!" he exclaimed as his dad placed the ruler on top of his head and then drew a mark on the wall with the pencil. Dad smiled and simply said, "We'll see."

Turning around with great expectation, Eric's smile vanished as he looked at the line his dad drew. Nothin.' He hadn't growed at all. Seeing his disappointment, Daddy wrapped his big, burly arms around Eric, gave him a hug and said, "It's OK, son; I bet you'll grow two feet next week!" Eric smiled and said, "Oh, Daddy, I already have two feet!"

Holy Growth Chart, Batman!

When a child is born, that baby is expected to grow and develop. At the time of this writing, we have been blessed with three new babies added to the family (a set of twin girls, and a boy). I love sitting in the rocking chair while holding my grandchildren in my arms, talking to them, singing to them as I give them a bottle, and then watching them smile at me (okay, I know it's just gas, but I still love those smiles). But to be honest, I'm looking forward with great anticipation to the day when I will no longer hear the words, "Grandpa will change your diaper!"

I can't wait for the time when I can sit on the couch with my grandkids snuggled up next to me while I read them a book, or take them out on a Grandpa-date so we can have a McWonderful time. I get excited when I think about throwing a Frisbee or football with them in the back yard. I'm especially pumped about the prospect of going to their ball games or band concerts to cheer for them. But all of that is contingent upon one very crucial thing—their growth. They must grow up some before those things can happen.

My grandchildren see their pediatrician regularly. The doctor checks their vitals, examines their bodies, pushes here and wiggles there, measures this and weighs that, all for the purpose of ensuring they are growing as they should. Praise the Lord, they are presently developing and growing exactly as anticipated. However, at the first sign of something wrong, I know their parents will have them right there in the doctor's office, seeking guidance and help.

Now, if human parents and grandparents are that concerned about the growth of their kids, is it any wonder that your Heavenly Father is concerned about your spiritual growth as well? To be a Super Man of God, you must continuously grow in your relationship with Him. No two ways about it. And to grow, you must eat—eat properly, that is.

From Milk to Meat

It makes sense that an infant can feed only on milk, right? There's nothing wrong with me holding my infant granddaughter in my arms while giving her a bottle. But what about my nine-year-old grandson? Something would be drastically wrong if his mommy were still rocking him in her arms while feeding him a bottle of warm milk. It's expected that by now he has grown to the point where he can handle eating meat, potatoes and those ever-so-yummy vegetables.

God's Word plays a vital role in your spiritual growth. Listen, my friend, your Bible is a book to be eaten and digested, not just read and understood. To be a Super Man of God you need to *grow up!*[2] And to grow up healthy, you need to feed on God's Word daily.

Give it Some Thought

- Below is a "Growth Chart." Take the time to look up the passages of Scripture, then write your observations and plan of action—what are you going to do about it?

Give Him your heart and mind—read Proverbs 23:19, 26; 4:23; 28:26; and Matthew 22:37.
  • How am I going to do this?

Read the Bible daily—read Romans 15:4; Proverbs 4:13; Psalm 32:8; Matthew 4:4; and 2 Timothy 3:16-17.
  • How am I going to do this?

Obey whatever God reveals to you—read John 14:15, 23; 1 John 2:4-5, 5:3.
  • How am I going to do this?

Work out your faith—read Philippians 1:27, 2:12; Galatians 6:7-9; Hebrews 12:1; and 1 Peter 2:12.
  • How am I going to do this?

I challenge you to 1) pick at least one verse from each category above and memorize it; and 2) make the time to dig deeper into each of the four concepts above.

Week 4, Day 4

Now, I know he's not a superhero, so in that sense he has no business being in a study with Superman as our main character, but I like Winnie the Pooh[3]—I always have. Winnie comes up with some of the most fanciful comments that just tickle my mental funny bone, probably because they hit so close to home. For example, here are some great Winnie-isms:
  • "People say nothing is impossible, but I do nothing every day."
  • "I wasn't going to eat it; I was just going to taste it."
  • "Could you spare a small smackerel? I feel rumbly in my tumbly."
  • And my most favorite: "Oh, bother."

So why the nostalgic trip deep into the 100-Acre-Wood? Because of one of Pooh's most endearing statements, whenever he's gotten himself into a pickle and needs to figure a way out. He plops himself on the ground, crosses his arms across his chest, squeezes his eyes shut and wrinkles up his nose. Then, tapping himself on the side of his head he says, "Think, think, think." When you find yourself in a tough spot, what do you tend to "think, think, think" about?

A Penny for Your Thoughts
Have you ever stood at a wishing well and, just for the fun of it, tossed in an old, dirty penny? Think of that well as your mind. What's being tossed into it? What are other people tossing in there? What are you

allowing to enter your mind every day? What are you allowing yourself to think about?

Imagine you are living in a remote village where your only source of water is a single well just on the outskirts of town. The climate is hot, dry and unfriendly. You have no other resource for water, so you desperately need that well. The nearest neighboring village is over one hundred miles away on foot through arid, dangerous wasteland—a trek you dare not take.

Without the fresh water in your well, you and everyone in your village would surely die. Suddenly that well becomes extremely important, doesn't it? The water it contains is now worth more than all the gold, silver and precious stones in the world combined.

In addition, imagine that just outside of your village is your archenemy, intent on your total annihilation. The leader of that demonic army will stop at nothing to see you dead, or at the very least weak and sickly—totally unable to defend yourself, completely vulnerable to his every attack.

Rarely does he try frontal assaults, as he knows you will stand firm, holding your ground, determined not to give him even an inch. However, by using guerilla warfare he effectively erodes your resistance. Again and again he peppers you with ambushes, sabotage, mini-raids, petty annoyances and hit-and-run tactics.

His goal: poison the well—that precious well from which you draw life. He knows it cannot be too much poison all at once, nor too powerful, otherwise you might detect it. No, he's just going to add a drop tonight, and then another drop in about a week or so. Maybe two drops the following week. Just enough to taint the water and make you sick.

Proverbs 23:26
"My son, give me your heart, and let your eyes observe my ways."

Your enemy is coy, he's subtle, and his methods are surprisingly simple. First he walks up to you, dressed like one of your neighbors or co-workers, and engages you in idle conversation that goes nowhere, and yet seems to take your full attention. You talk about the weather, you discuss the latest movies, and you even talk about religion. As he tells you a joke that's just a bit off-color, you don't see him reach behind your back and drop a pellet of something evil into the well. A few moments later he abruptly ends the conversation with a friendly smile and walks away.

On another day he saunters up to you in the form of a woman. Oh, not in an erotic way, but subtly provocative. He knows if he were to overdo it, you'd be suspicious. So, her top reveals just a slight amount of her cleavage; you barely catch a hint of her perfume. Her eyes seem to suck you right in, and her smile makes you melt. As you blush in her presence, fumbling for the right words to say, you never notice her tip a vial of some wicked concoction into your well. You don't hear it hiss as it hits the water.

Yet another time he comes up to you like an old friend, familiar and yet somehow not. He begins to tell you a story. You picture in your mind's eye the action as he describes the chase; you feel the emotion as he tells of a love lost. You cringe at some of the strong language he uses, but you dismiss it as being part of the storyline. Enthralled in the exploits of the hero and the drama surrounding the heroine, you don't even notice that he sat, rather comfortably, on the edge of the well. As his story focuses on a bedroom scene where the actors are romantically enjoying each other's company, he lets slip from his grasp a pale, innocent-looking powder into the water.

Day after day, week after week, he approaches you in various ingeniously-crafted disguises. Some of them you've become familiar with, even friendly. You never suspect anything is wrong. Yet, as you daily drink from that well, the poisoned water slowly begins to do its work.

Your body starts to weaken—imperceptibly at first, but you feel more and more fatigued. Your vision becomes a bit blurred. Your response time slows. You become lethargic, melancholy, and can't seem to make yourself care about things that once seemed important. Your thinking is a bit confused at times and you find your attention drawn away to other things. Your priorities have changed. You've forgotten why you are wearing that heavy, cumbersome armor. Fighting the battle just doesn't seem as important anymore.

As time progresses and you go through your daily routines, you find yourself looking forward to his visits. In fact, when you see him approaching, you lean your sword against the side of the well and greet him with a smile. Taking off your helmet and setting it on the ground next to your breastplate, you embrace him warmly. He's become like an old friend, a glove that fits ever so comfortably. He hands you a chocolate-chip cookie, freshly baked, laced with more of his poison. You wash it down with a huge gulp of tainted well water. His task is nearly complete, his goal almost accomplished.

Don't Taint the Water

Think about what you just read. We watched as the enemy repeatedly used skilled and proven tactics to achieve his devious goal. We know how vital that water supply is; and we understand the essential, vital importance of guarding that well at all costs. And yet we let down our guard.

You and I also have a well. That well contains something that directly affects our health—our spiritual health. You only have one well, and what comes out of it determines the quality and character of your life. We must guard that well at all costs.[4] We must always and ever keep that which is in the well pure, because our enemy's mission is to taint that well and ruin our lives. You need to keep it safe, not allowing *anything* to enter it that would poison you.

Give it Some Thought

- Read 2 Corinthians 11:3; Matthew 13:39; and 1 Peter 5:8. Who wants to taint your well (mind)?

- Read Matthew 13:25. When does the enemy attack you? ("When I'm sleeping" isn't an acceptable answer—be more specific.) How does he attack? ("Sowing weeds"—again, be more specific; consider Galatians 5:9 in your answer.)

- Read 1 Peter 5:8; James 4:7; Ephesians 6:11 and 4:27. What does God expect us to do when the enemy attacks our well (mind)?

All this week we've been talking about a super meal for a Super Man. What are you eating spiritually? How often are you eating, and what are you feeding upon? Whatever it is, it's being put into your well (mind).

If your well is polluted, it WILL have a direct impact on your attitudes, behavior, and your speech—in other words, every aspect of your life. Your heart is the wellspring of life itself. Pollute the well and you pollute everything that comes out of it. So don't taint the water!

Week 4, Day 5

These guys were inseparable, best friends. Danny, Niah, Misha and Az grew up in the palace together. They loved running through the halls playing tag, or hide-and-seek, or "freak out Az," as Niah used to call it. Now that they were teens, those games were left far behind them. Girls were all the rage. And oh, the fun they had sneaking mice into a girl's room, then waiting to hear her scream.

One morning just before sunrise, Danny awoke in a cold sweat. What he thought was just a nightmare full of clanging swords and blood-curdling screams had become a terrifying reality. The palace was being invaded! Within seconds his friends gathered in his room, wondering what they should do.

Suddenly the door opened and one of the palace guards appeared. "Sires," he said, "stay right here, latch the door behind me and don't open it for anyone!"

"What's going on?" Misha shouted, but the guard had already left. Terrified, Az ran to the door and slid the steel bar across the latch, sealing them in.

Later that night the four friends lay their heads down on a strange pillow, under strange blankets on a strange bed in a strange room. Closing his eyes, Danny tried to review in his head the events that put him and his friends in this horrible place. The palace had been overrun, the guards slain, the King taken, and Danny and his friends captured. All in all, not a very good day. The sounds coming from outside their door were bizarre and ugly. Men spoke in a language they did not understand.

Do We Do, or Do We Don't?
Days later, in a palace in a new land, an official looking guy with red plumes on his shoulder pads and a weird crest emblazoned on his chest came into their room and introduced himself as Ashpenaz. At least, that's what Danny thought he said; the language was so hard to understand.

Ashpenaz explained to them that the reason their lives had been spared was because his King, the glorious and all-powerful Nebuchadnezzar, had chosen them to become servants in his palace. Tomorrow morning would start their training. In the meantime, a feast had been prepared for them—in their honor. As the servants set the food on the table, Ashpenaz explained to them that this was a high privilege being given them. The meat, a delicacy in their land, had just been offered in sacrifice to Nabu. This indeed was a rare thing that the King was doing.

Danny had to think fast. Meat offered to Nabu? Was that a person? A god? Should they eat it? It looked fantastic and smelled even better. His stomach growled, and he could feel his saliva glands working overtime. Glancing over at his friends, he could see the wide-eyed looks and growing smiles on their faces.

Something deep inside him stirred. Something was telling him not to eat. Was the meat poisoned? That didn't make sense. Why would the King capture them just to poison them? No, this feeling was something different.

Then it hit him. To eat that meat would be to acknowledge that Nabu was God. They might be captives in a foreign country, there against their will; and they might be stuck in this place for a very long time, but that didn't give them an excuse to forsake the true God and go against His will for their lives. God had to have a reason for allowing them to be there. They might never know what that reasoning might be, but that didn't matter. This wasn't about them.

> # Luke 4:8
> *"And Jesus answered him, 'It is written, 'You shall worship the Lord your God, and him only shall you serve.'"*

Danny turned to Ashpenaz and, to everyone's shock, told the King's chief official, "Thank you, but no thank you." Seeing the surprise on Ashpenaz's face, and the disappointment on his friends' Danny continued. "Sir, we respectfully decline your offer. You see, we worship the one true God whose name is Elohim. It is the conviction of our hearts that if we eat anything that has been offered to another god, it will defile us—making us dirty in the eyes of the one true God."

Ashpenaz looked like a deer caught in the torchlight. He didn't know what to say or do. His mouth just hung open, unable to form any words. Finally, shaking his head he said, "No one has ever rejected the King's meat before. This is unheard of. If I don't feed you this meal —if you don't eat this food to build up your strength—the King will have my head!"

Danny paused, thinking carefully how to phrase what was going on in his mind. Praying to God for help he said, "With all due respect, I would like to suggest a compromise. For the next ten days, feed us nothing but vegetables and water. At the end of the ten days, check in to see how we're doing. If our health and well-being have declined, then you can do with us whatever you want."

It was totally out of character for Ashpenaz, but he was starting to like these guys, so he agreed. For the next ten days those boys ate nothing but vegetables and drank nothing but water. They would sit at their table, watching the other captives chowing down on the most mouthwatering dishes they had ever seen, while they gnawed away at raw carrots and leeks. They sipped at their glasses of water while the others chugged the King's choice wines. They were the objects of ridicule, yet they continued to grow healthier and were better nourished than any of the other captives.

At the end of the ten days, Ashpenaz was totally floored. He had no clue how they had done it, but those four boys were not only better physically than the rest, but they caught on to the language faster, understood all the literature they were reading, and Danny seemed to excel the most. Who woulda thunk that a veggie platter could do all that?

Give it Some Thought

- Read Daniel 1:1-21. Daniel and friends were put into a terrible situation, with no way out. No one would have blamed them for caving under the pressure to conform to the environment in which they were placed. But Daniel held his ground. Why did Daniel refuse to eat the king's meat?

- In a very real sense, Daniel was an alien in a foreign land. As a son of God, you too are an alien in a foreign land. What is some of this world's "food" that you need to abstain from, and why?

- What was so "magical" about eating vegetables and water? What was it that really set Daniel and his friends apart?

- How can you apply that to your life—what "vegetables and water" should you be feeding upon?

- Challenge (I triple-dog dare you): for the next ten days, separate yourself from all "foreign food" (e.g., television) and instead, "feed" upon God's Word. Are you man enough? Oooooh, was that below the belt?

- At your next meeting, share with the guys how you are doing with the above challenge.

"Let your light shine before others, so that they may see your good works and give glory to your Father who is in heaven."
Matthew 5:16

Week 5
Will the Real Super Man Please Stand Up?

Week 5, Day 1

Clark Kent, Bruce Wayne, Peter Parker, Barry Allen and Tony Starke are names that mean nothing to the enemy. However, the names Superman, Batman, Spiderman, The Flash, Iron Man, even Captain America and The Green Lantern, are just a few of the names that have struck fear into the hearts of such archvillains as Lex Luthor, the Joker, the Green Goblin, Red Skull and the Mandarin. (Seriously, who comes up with these names?)

What does the name *(insert your name here)* do to the heart of your spiritual enemy? Truth be told, absolutely nothing. Your earth-name has no bearing on what the archvillain of your soul does or does not do. However, as a Super Man of God, you do bear a name that is greatly feared by the enemy. As a born-again Christian, you bear the Heavenly name Teknon Theos (and no, I'm not making that up; in the Greek it stands for "Child of God").[1]

Guys, that name represents a high and holy calling. You see, that name is not given to just anyone. There is a certain criterion that must be met before ever being given the name Child of God.[2] Once you have met God's condition, your purpose in life is then to draw the attention of those around you to the Almighty, all-powerful God of the Universe.[3]

- Why should we draw attention to God?

- How should we do that?

- How are you doing that?

Is the life you're building pointing others to Christ? God, and God alone, is worthy "to receive glory and honor and power."[4] It's not about you, nor is it about me. The Apostle Paul put it this way: "From *him* and through *him* and to *him* are all things. To *him* (belongs) the glory forever" (Romans 11:36, emphasis mine).[5]

But why? Why is God alone worthy of *all* glory and honor? Consider this (if possible, read the following out loud—it's powerful):
- Only God is the first and the last—the beginning and the end.[6]
- Only God is the curator of creation and the architect of it all.[7]
- Only God always was, always is, and always will be.[8]
- He is the compassionate and gracious God, always slow to anger and abounding in love and faithfulness.[9]
- Only God is the source of eternal salvation; the author and finisher of your faith.[10]
- He alone is the bread of life.[11]
- He is the comforter,[12] the Counselor,[13] and the Chief Cornerstone.[14]
- He is the Father of glory,[15] the Father of lights,[16] the Righteous Father,[17] and a father to the fatherless.[18]
- He is *the* way, *the* truth and *the* life.[19]
- He is the eternal, immortal, invisible, and only wise King.[20]
- He is the God of Hosts;[21] the God of my salvation;[22] the God of all comfort;[23] the God of all grace;[24] the God of mercy;[25]

the God of peace;[26] the God of retribution;[27] and the God of truth.[28]

- He is the God who sees;[29] the God who forgives;[30] and the God who delivers me.[31]
- He is the Almighty,[32] All Knowing,[33] All Powerful,[34] and always present[35] God in my life.
- It is He who built all things;[36] He who forms the mountains and creates the wind;[37] He who blotted out my transgressions;[38] and it is He who comforts me.[39]
- He is the King of the Jews,[40] the King of the nations,[41] the King of all the earth,[42] the King of heaven,[43] the King of glory,[44] the King of kings,[45] and he is my king.[46]
- He is the Lord God Almighty;[47] the Lord Most High;[48] and the Lord who made heaven and earth.[49]
- He is the Lord our shield;[50] the Lord our God;[51] the Lord our Maker;[52] and the Lord our Righteousness.[53]
- He is the Lord of glory,[54] the Lord of Peace,[55] the Lord of the harvest,[56] and He is the Lord of Lords.[57]
- He is my all in all;[58] my rock, my fortress, my deliverer, my shield and my stronghold.[59]
- He is my God and my Father;[60] my ever present help;[61] my hiding place;[62] my hope;[63] and He is my redeemer.[64]
- To God alone I owe my respect, my honor, my praise, my worship, my attention, my service, my mind, my heart, my life and my all.

Wow! That's quite a list! Can you begin to understand why our Heavenly Father, the One and only True God, is more than worthy of all of our honor, praise, worship and glory? What a reason to stand up and shout out with everything you've got: "In my life, Lord, please be glorified today."

Now, I have an important question for you. Is that your heart's desire? Do you truly want to live a life that draws people to God? Take a moment and meditate on the verse at the beginning of this chapter. No matter what you do, when you do it, or where it's being done, always do it for God's glory. Always live in such a way that as people watch you, they see King Jesus and not King Me.

Just think about that. God is not expecting you to live a life that occasionally, or even mostly, glorifies Him. Every aspect of your life, every moment of every day, is to be lived in such a way that He (and He alone) receives recognition, praise and honor. When you live like that, you are being a Super Man of God.

Now that's a tall order. I mean, living a life that in every way and at all times glorifies God is certainly a noble and holy endeavor. But is it really possible? Can you actually function in a way that *every* thought, *every* word and *every* action is in *every* way reflecting to the world around you the absolute greatness, majesty, wonder and supremacy of the Almighty God of the Universe? My answer to you is yes—yes you can! Let me remind you that God will never command you to do something that is impossible to do. If He did, He would be setting you up to sin, and that's against God's nature.[65]

One of the biggest obstacles we face, preventing us from being Super Men of God, is believing the lie of the enemy that says, *"Well, you're only human, and that means you're going to sin."* Yes, we're human. Yes, we have a natural human tendency toward sin. But no, we do not have to give in to it. We sin because King Me is sitting on the throne of our hearts. We sin because we choose to. We do what we do because in our hearts we want what we want.

So what exactly do you want?

Give it Some Thought
- Read Romans 10:9-10; Ephesians 2:8-9; Acts 4:12 and 16:31. What is the requirement for receiving the name "Child of God"?

- Are you a child of God?

- What evidence is in your daily living that demonstrates your answer?

- As a group, let's take a few moments to share how you became a child of God (share your testimony of salvation).

- Read 1 Peter 1:15-16 and 1 Thessalonians 4:7-8. Is it possible, as a child of God, for you to be holy? If no—why not? If yes—how is that possible? (For help, see 2 Corinthians 7:1 and 2 Peter 1:3.)

- Read Micah 6:8. What three things does God require of us?

  - When something is required of you by God, what does that mean?

  - Why does God require those three things?

- What does a man look like who is walking with God?

- Does your answer above describe you?

- What is something you know God wants you to do, that you're not doing?

- Why aren't you doing this?

Week 5, Day 2

Okay, I know I'm taking a giant leap here. I understand that I'm doing the unspeakable by momentarily moving you from the world of DC Comics to the universe of George Lucas, but bear with me for a moment. There is a scene from *Star Wars: Episode V – The Empire Strikes Back*[66] where Luke Skywalker manages to escape Darth Vader's trap with an amazing acrobatic flip. In genuine surprise Vader says, "Impressive. Most impressive. Obi-Wan has taught you well." Then a few moments later Vader taunts Luke with the words, "The Force is with you, young Skywalker, but you are not a Jedi yet."

Just as Vader did with Luke, Satan wants to taunt you. He wants to distract and discourage you—to trap you. He tries to tell you that although God may be with you, you are not a Super Man yet. Don't listen to his lies. Don't get caught in his web of deceit. As a Christian, you already are a Super Man of God. Don't ever forget that your real identity is Teknon Theos—son of God.

- Do the people around you—your family, your friends, your co-workers and your neighbors—know who you really are?

- Are you living your life in such a way that it is standing up and standing out for Christ?

Okay, let's hop back into our trans-universe machine and go back to the world of DC Comics. As a kid growing up, I loved Monday nights because I was allowed to stay up so I could watch reruns of *The Amazing Adventures of Superman*.[67] Every week actor George Reeves would don the blue tights and red cape and soar through the air, saving damsels in distress while giving the bad guy the pounding he deserved. Every week, the show would open with Superman flying through the sky. Onlookers would shout out, "Look, up in the sky! It's a bird! It's a plane! No, it's Superman!"

---

1 Peter 2:9

"But you are a chosen people, a royal priesthood, a holy nation, a people belonging to God, that you may declare the praises of him who called you out of darkness into his wonderful light."

In the same way, the people with whom you rub shoulders every day should see your life and say "Look! It's a Super Man of God!" But how does that happen? Do you have to wear red tighties over blue spandex and have a huge **S** (for Saved, Sanctified or Saint—take your pick) emblazoned on your chest? Nah. Although it would definitely cause you to stand out in a crowd, that's just not practical (nor is it the kind of attention God wants you to get).

Here's a question for you to consider: As people watch you, are they getting a right view of God? Are you making a lasting impression upon them for the Kingdom of Heaven? In fact, there's a deeper, more significant question you should be asking yourself. Do those people even know that they should be asking you to tell them who you really are and how you're able to do the things you do for Christ?

The only way that answer can be "yes" is if you are living every moment of every day as a Super Man of God. If they can't see your real identity, then they will never ask you to explain to them who you are and how you're able to do the things you do. You will never be able to point them to Christ.

> ## 1 Peter 3:15
> *"In your hearts set apart Christ as Lord. Always be prepared to give an answer to everyone who asks you to give the reason for the hope that you have. But do this with gentleness and respect."*

Guys, I can't help but wonder if we have missed the most important part of this verse. Too often we emphasize the section that says we need to be ready to give an answer to anyone who asks us why we believe what we believe. While it is true that we need to be prepared to share our faith with the world around us, and while it is also very important to give the reason for the hope we have, this is not the key point of the verse.

The most significant part of this verse is found in the words, "In your hearts set apart Christ as Lord." You see, until you set apart (or sanctify) your heart, until you dedicate yourself completely to God, your life will be no different than the rest of the world around you. If you're not living a life set apart for God, how will anyone know to ask you why your life is so different?

Let me state the obvious here: You are not Clark Kent. But you are also not _(insert your earth-name here)_. You are Teknon Theos—son of God. So live like it!

Give it Some Thought

- How would you define "lordship"? What does it look like?

- How does one "set apart Christ as Lord of his life"?

- What are some of the characteristics of someone who is living with Christ as their Lord?

  - Are you showing those characteristics?

Week 5, Day 3

As people watch your life, they *are* seeing how you view God. Good or bad, your daily life is showing to others who God is to you. How you relate to and interact with God on a daily basis will be reflected in every word you speak and everything you do.

What are your family, friends, co-workers and neighbors understanding about God as they listen to your words and observe your actions? Are you a mirror reflecting Him, or a wall hiding Him? Do you let your light shine for all to see, or are you hiding it somewhere deep within?

In Scripture God is often referred to as "the God of Abraham" (see Genesis 24:12, 26:24; 28:13-15; and 31:42). He is called "the God of Jacob" (see Psalm 20:1; 46:7; 75:9 and 76:6). He's identified in some passages as "the God of Elijah" (2 Kings 2:14), and "the God of your fathers Abraham, Isaac and Jacob" (see Exodus 3:6, 16-17; 4:5; Matthew 22:32; Mark 12:26-27 and Luke 20:37-38). In each instance, whenever He revealed Himself in that way, the people responded in total awe.
* If God were to reveal Himself to your family and friends as the God of *(insert your name)*, what kind of God would they see? How would they respond?

Here's the bottom line: when we set apart Christ as Lord in our hearts, He will be seen as Lord in our lives. That is when the real Super Man of God begins to stand up and stand out.

In Conclusion
In Chapter One we got a glimpse into parts of Solomon's journal as he wrote about his failed attempts to find meaning and purpose to his life. Do you remember how he ended his account? He wrote, "Now all has been heard; here is the conclusion of the matter: Fear God and keep his commandments, for this is the whole duty of man. For God

will bring every deed into judgment, including every hidden thing, whether it is good or evil" (Ecclesiastes 12:13-14).

What a powerful conclusion! What a point for us to seriously apply to our own lives. Solomon's painful discovery can be our opportunity to learn and grow.[68] Meaning and purpose to life is found only when we focus our entire being around glorifying God. No matter what you're doing, when you're doing it, how you're doing it or why you're doing it, God is always to be glorified.[69]

Never forget that God formed you, He made you, He created you for His glory.[70] Glorifying God has been programmed into your very DNA. Are you functioning according to The Manufacturer's specs? Are you living a life that glorifies Him?[71] Are you daily walking in complete surrender[72] and total obedience to your Heavenly Father at all times?[73] Only then will you glorify Him. Only then will you find genuine satisfaction and fulfillment in life. Only then will you be a Super Man of God!

Read the words of 1 Corinthians 10:31. "So whether you eat or drink or whatever you do, do it all for the glory of God." Okay, now here's a simple yet very important question for you: According to that verse, how much of your life is to glorify God? The answer: all of it. Every bit of it. Focus on that word "all" for a moment. How would you define it? What does "all" mean exactly? Let me share with you a very simple definition. Hold on to your seat because this is going to blow you away with its profoundness: "all" means all and that's all "all" means! Mind blowing!

God is always all about His glory—not ours. He says, "For my own sake, for my own sake I do this. How can I let myself be defamed? I will not yield my glory to another" (Isaiah 48:11). When we seek our own praise and glory, we are dethroning God and setting up King Me in His place. God will not tolerate that. "I am the Lord; that is my name! I will not give my glory to another or my praise to idols" (Isaiah 42:8).

Colossians 3:23

"Whatever you do, work heartily, as for the Lord and not for men."

Whatever you do, guys, *whatever* you do—it doesn't matter whether it's your actions or your words—make sure you always do them in a way that gives attention to God.[74] Nowhere in Scripture will you find a verse that says, "Oh, dear Christian, it sure would be nice if you would try your best to glorify God more often than not in your life." No way!

You will, however, find the Biblical principle that *everything* you say, and *everything* you do in life is to be said and done in Jesus' name! Not just some of the things you say and most of the things you do, but everything. To be a real Super Man of God, each and every individual word you say, as well as each and every particular activity you do—all of it, every part of it—must always be said and done to the glory of God. If they are not glorifying Him, you are sinning.

Let's be real. How often do you closely examine your words and actions—before ever speaking them or doing them—to make sure that each and every one glorifies God? OK, I know that one was below the belt; yet that is what we are commanded to do.

Give it Some Thought
- Read Psalm 115:1 and Revelation 4:11. What does it mean to glorify God?

- Why does God want us to glorify Him?

- What are some ways in which we can glorify God? (For help see Psalm 96:1-9; Matthew 5:16; 1 Peter 1:14-15 and John 14:15.)

- Name some ways we might steal the glory from God.

Week 5, Day 4

In the late 1970s and early '80s, a brokerage firm named E.F. Hutton put together an advertising campaign that had everyone talking (or maybe I should say "listening"). In their television commercials you would see two people out for a jog, or riding a train; possibly at a dinner party or even conversing in the middle of a Broadway show. In every scenario, the crowd or activity happening around them was noisy. As the two individuals talked, their conversation began to focus on the stock market. Inevitably one person would say to the other, "Well, my broker is E.F. Hutton. And E.F. Hutton says …"

Those words were apparently very magical. Once uttered, the rest of the world fell totally silent. Joggers stopped in mid-stride. Commuters on the train put down their newspapers. Dinner guests stopped passing the mashed potatoes. Even the actors on stage halted their scene. Everyone's attention was drawn to that conversation because everyone wanted to hear the sage advice of the legendary E.F. Hutton. Every commercial always ended with the same powerful tagline: "When E.F. Hutton speaks, people listen."

Well, when you or I talk, the rest of the world may not come to a screeching halt just to hear what we have to say, but the people around us are listening. So what are they hearing?

What's That You Say?
Listen carefully to the words of Paul in Colossians 3:17.

> "Whatever (we) do, whether in word or deed, (we are to) do it all in the name of the Lord Jesus, giving thanks to God the Father through Him."

Notice that Paul uses the word "whatever." Whatever you may say, whatever words come out of your mouth at any given moment—no matter to whom you're speaking or the reason for your words—always make sure you're saying them in a way that glorifies God.[75]

Why? Why should I be so careful about what I say? What's wrong with spouting off when I get hot under the collar? Why can't I colorfully express my opinion? To answer, let's pause for a brief moment here and take a quick stroll through the book of Proverbs. On this little walk, I want you to notice along the way what God says about the words that come out of your mouth.

- "When words are many, sin is not absent, but he who holds his tongue is wise." (Proverbs 10:19)
- "Reckless words pierce like a sword, but the tongue of the wise brings healing." (Proverbs 12:18)
- "He who guards his lips guards his life, but he who speaks rashly will come to ruin." (Proverbs 13:13)
- "The tongue of the wise commends knowledge, but the mouth of the fool gushes folly." (Proverbs 15:2)
- "The tongue that brings healing is a tree of life, but a deceitful tongue crushes the spirit." (Proverbs 15:14)
- "A wise man's heart guides his mouth, and his lips promote instruction. Pleasant words are a honeycomb, sweet to the soul." (Proverbs 16:23-24)
- "A man of knowledge uses words with restraint." (Proverbs 17:27a)
- "Even a fool is thought wise if he keeps silent, and discerning if he holds his tongue." (Proverbs 17:28)
- "He who guards his mouth and his tongue keeps himself from calamity." (Proverbs 21:23)
- "A word aptly spoken is like apples of gold in settings of silver." (Proverbs 25:11)

Always consider what you say, my friend—God does. Every time you open your mouth to speak, before a single word comes out, ask God to "set a guard over (your) mouth" and "keep watch over the door of (your) lips" (Psalm 141:3). Cry out to Him, "Father, please 'let the words of my mouth and the meditation of my heart be pleasing in your sight, O Lord, my Rock and my Redeemer'" (Psalm 19:14). Why is that so important, you ask? There is coming a day when every one of us "will have to give account on the Day of Judgment for *every* careless word (we) have spoken" (Matthew 12:36).

To be honest, our tendency at this point is to think, *"EVERY word, EVERY moment of EVERY day? C'mon dude, you're asking the impossible. I speak thousands of words daily! It just can't be done."* I agree with you—without God's help, it is utterly impossible. However, let me remind you that with God nothing is impossible.[76] He will always give you exactly what you need, when you need, it to accomplish everything He has commanded you to do! God doesn't want you to fail, so you can rest assured that any command He gives you—through His strength and guidance, you can do it![77]

> ## Ephesians 4:29
> *"Let no corrupting talk come out of your mouths, but only such as is good for building up, as fits the occasion, that it may give grace to those who hear."*

Our problem lies in the fact that we are used to talking without putting much thought into what we're saying. Or, when we do think through what we're going to say, glorifying God with our words isn't top on our priority list. So, the concept of thinking through everything you say before you speak so that your words bring honor to God feels very foreign. The exciting thing is, God has created us as creatures of habit. Repetitive action eventually forms habitual action. Yes, it's work now, but it won't always be.

With God's help you can "keep (your) tongue from evil and (your) lips from deceitful speech" (1 Pet. 3:10). It truly is possible to consistently restrain your tongue from saying things that will not glorify God.

In Matthew 12:34 Jesus is talking to the Pharisees about the sinful condition of their hearts. In that verse He makes a very interesting statement. He says, "Out of the overflow of the heart the mouth speaks." As He's talking about the "heart," He isn't referring to that muscle in your chest that goes thumpity-thump. No, He's speaking about the core of who you are. It is "command central." It's the place where your thoughts, passions, desires, will, and decision-making all occur. In other words, your mind.

93

Your words are a direct result of what is going on in your thoughts. What you think will come out in what you say. If your thoughts are focused on King Me, your words will be centered on self. The prophet Isaiah said that the man whose mind is busy with evil will speak folly[78] On the flip side, if your thoughts are focused on God, your words will draw attention to Him.

I challenge you to ask yourself—and answer honestly—this question: Does each and every word I speak and the motivation behind them bring glory to God? When I am speaking to my spouse, to my children, to my employer or employees, to my co-workers, to my family members, to my friends and neighbors, even to those annoying telemarketers, am I considering carefully everything I am saying to be sure each and every word is glorifying God? Since your words reveal what is in your thoughts, the real question is: Do your thoughts truly glorify God?

Give it Some Thought
- Read Ephesians 4:29; Matthew 12:36; Psalm 19:14; Proverbs 15:1, 4; 16:24 and 18:21.

   - Why are our words so powerful?

   - Why do my words matter to God?

- Read Psalm 141:3; Proverbs 17:27, 21:23; and Colossians 3:8. How can I control my tongue?

Week 5, Day 5

When the comic book character affectionately known as Superman was created back in 1938, the goal was for the man of steel to be the ideal American—one who always stood for truth, justice and the American way.

Superman is famous not only for his supernatural strength and amazing abilities, he is also known for his humility and genuine concern for helping others. He is modest, courteous and always tries to do the right thing. His compassion for others even goes out to those who don't deserve it. All in all, he's a pretty good guy.

What does Superman do? I mean, of course he flies around keeping airplanes from crashing and school buses from falling off of really tall bridges … but how many times a day does that really happen?

As a Super Man of God, What Do *You* Do?
One hundred guys surveyed, the top three answers are on the board (not really; I just always wanted to say that). That's an important question to consider. What are you doing for God? A typical response to that question may be something like, "Oh, I volunteer to help out in the nursery at church, and I've even gone on a couple of short-term missions trips. My small group went out last week and raked an elderly neighbor's leaves, and I am a volunteer Chaplain's assistant at our local jail."

Now, don't misunderstand me here. Those are some great things you can do for the Kingdom. But what about the things you do on a daily basis? What about the mundane, non-spiritual things you do every day? Did you ever stop to consider the fact that even those things should be done in a way that glorifies God?

As we will see later on in our study, Superman is always Superman. Even as Clark Kent, he never stops being Superman. You, too, are always Teknon Theos. Even in your normal, everyday, run-of-the-mill life you never stop being a child of God. So, what do you do?

Simple things like taking out the trash, filling the car with gas, mowing your yard or snow blowing the driveway are all things that should glorify God. Oh, now here's where I start meddling, because even crossing your arms to make a point, rolling your eyes, sighing loudly, or offering a friendly pat on the back for encouragement; the raising of an eyebrow, a shrug of your shoulders, the glaring of your eyes, the shaking of your head, or a simple smile of encouragement is considered by God to be a deed that should be done in a way that glorifies Him. Seriously! Hey, dude—don't shoot the messenger.

> ## Colossians 3:17
> *"Whatever (we) do, whether in word or deed, (we are to) do it all in the name of the Lord Jesus, giving thanks to God the Father through Him." (Compare with 1 Corinthians 10:31)*

Although God cares deeply about the things you do to and around others, He is also very interested in each and every thing you do even in private. In the times when no one is around, the times when you think you're completely alone, God sees it all and will bring every deed into judgment—including every hidden thing, good or bad.[79]

So here's the question again: As a Super Man of God, what are you doing? Nothing, absolutely *nothing* we do is covered up that will not one day be revealed. Nothing we do is so well hidden that it will not be made known. Even the words you quietly whisper in secret will be loudly heard—as if you were standing on top of your roof, shouting it out at the top of your lungs.[80] You see, God's "eyes are on all (our) ways; they are not hidden from (Him), nor is (our) sin concealed from (His) eyes" (Jeremiah 16:17, additions mine; compare with Psalm 90:8, Hebrews 4:13).

Give it Some Thought
- Read 1 Samuel 2:3. Now read it again, and consider that verse carefully. God knows each and every one of your deeds, public and private. But this verse reveals something more, something much deeper. God not only knows all your deeds, but He knows the motivation of your heart behind each deed. He not only knows what you did, He also knows why you did it. Paul warns us that God "will bring to light what is hidden in darkness and will expose the *motives* of men's hearts" (1 Corinthians 4:5). We do what we do because in our hearts we

want what we want. What does your heart want? Does it want to glorify God, or to please self?

- Read Jeremiah 17:10. On the scales of God's justice your deeds are seriously considered, but God places more weight on your heart's motivation, on the thoughts you were thinking as you did each deed. Look again at that verse. God searches your heart and *examines your mind*.[81] Yes, your deeds are important to God, but even more important is the reason behind them—that which was going on in your thoughts as you did them. And He is not going to reward your deed, no matter how great it might be, if the thoughts and motivation behind it were wrong. What you think will become what you do. In order for your deeds and actions to glorify God, your thoughts must glorify Him.

- Share with the guys at least one takeaway you received this week, and what you plan to do about it.

*"Since we are surrounded by so great a cloud of witnesses,
let us also lay aside every weight, and sin which clings so closely,
and let us run with endurance the race that is set before us."*
Hebrews 12:1

Week 6
Oh, That Stupid Kryptonite!

Week 6, Day 1

Let me quickly review the whole Superman and Kryptonite thing. In the not-too-distant past, a horrible disaster happened that would forever alter the universe as we know it. Located only 50 light-years from earth (or approximately 300 trillion miles away—that's a bit of a drive) was a large planet called Krypton. The Kryptonians were an advanced race of kind and amazing people. However, a little over 35 earth-years ago, a massive explosion at that planet's core caused its total destruction. The planet Krypton and its people are no more.

Fortunately, that catastrophe was foreseen by a Kryptonian diplomat and scientist named Jor-El. Desperate to save his son, Jor-El created a spaceship big enough to hold his baby boy—sending him from that world just before their planet blew to smithereens. How lucky for us! For that very boy became the superhero we know today as Superman. (Spoiler alert: just to be sure we're clear, Superman is a fictitious character and not a real alien—sad fact.)

However, as that space cradle rocketed toward Earth with little Kal-El tucked away safely inside, it pulled along with it various chunks of the now-dead planet Krypton. When Kal-El's ship crash-landed just outside of Smallville, Kansas, those radioactive fragments—which would later be identified as Kryptonite—also landed, scattered randomly all over Earth.

As Kal-El (a.k.a. Clark Kent) grew up under the loving care of his adoptive parents, Jonathan and Martha Kent, he discovered that he had been gifted with amazing superpowers. His great speed, the ability to fly as well as bend steel with his bare hands—along with the all the other remarkable things he could do—were possible only because of his close proximity to Earth's yellow sun.

Then one day as he was flying to the rescue following a volcanic eruption, he encountered a piece of Kryptonite—a green, glowing rock which made him feel strange, fragile, and powerless. In that weakened condition he was completely vulnerable to the attacks of his enemies. You see, the poisonous radiation from that small piece of Superman's past somehow blocked the powerful effects of Earth's sun.

---

2 Corinthians 12:9-10

"But he said to me, 'My grace is sufficient for you, for my power is made perfect in weakness.' Therefore I will boast all the more gladly of my weaknesses, so that the power of Christ may rest upon me. For the sake of Christ, then, I am content with weaknesses, insults, hardships, persecutions, and calamities. For when I am weak, then I am strong."

Whenever Superman is around a chunk of Kryptonite, he is robbed of the strength the sun provides him. Oh, that stupid Kryptonite. (Another spoiler alert: there are no actual pieces of Kryptonite lying around planet Earth, as there never was a literal planet called Krypton —hopefully you're not too disappointed.)

Just like Superman, as Teknon Theos (a child of God) your power to stand firm against the enemy and effectively live a life that honors and glorifies God comes directly from the Son. The closer you are in your relationship to Jesus Christ, the greater your power. (By the way: unlike Kal-El, you really are a Super Man and not a fictitious character —just thought you'd want to know.)

- Read Philippians 4:13; 2 Peter 1:3; 2 Corinthians 12:9 and Ephesians 3:16. Why does a closer relationship with Christ increase your "power"?

- Why do we need that power?

Yet you too have a weakness. Don't deny it—you know it's true. There is something that can take you down without any warning. It's *your* Kryptonite. It's that radioactive element of your past life (before Christ). It's that temptation and sin you used to enjoy, that now constantly hounds you. It's that habitual, self-centered action that so easily trips you. Maybe it's a lustful thought, a lazy streak, a flare of anger or even a hint of pride. It could be a piece of triple chocolate cake or a can of beer; a cigarette or a desire to cut corners at work to save some bucks. The enemy knows what that is and he skillfully uses it to his advantage. Whatever your Kryptonite may be, it's a chunk from the planet of King Me. And it's nasty. Oh, that stupid Kryptonite.

Before we can move any further in this study, it is vitally important that we get this point. To know genuine victory in our battles against evil—to live lives that truly glorify our Heavenly Father—we must begin with the fact that even as sons of God, our tendency is to give in to temptation and choose to sin.

Believe me, I know. For years I focused all of my attention on changing outwardly. I tried to behave the way I thought I knew God wanted me to. I tried to live a life that impressed everyone around me with the things I knew about God and godliness. During that time in my life I struggled with the constantly nagging feeling of defeat and failure. I repetitively cycled through playing with my Kryptonite → sinning → confessing → playing with my Kryptonite → sinning →

confessing; over and over again. No more! Once I finally faced my Kryptonite and identified it for what it was, I could develop a plan to stay far away from it. You can too!

For the rest of this week and into the next we are going to talk about our Kryptonite. As long as King Me is sitting on the throne of our hearts, everything we think, say and do will be for the benefit of King Me! That's our Kryptonite. That's the one thing that constantly gets between us and the Son. That is the poisonous radiation that drains us of our supernatural ability to stand against the attacks of the enemy. King Me needs to be dethroned and deposed. He needs to come off the throne of your heart finally and for good!

So I challenge you to stop right here, right now, and pray. Ask God to help you identify your Kryptonite. Ask Him to reveal to you the areas of your life where King Me has taken over. Then ask Him to help you be His Man of Steel as you face down the enemy. Remember, through Christ you can live a consistent godly life! You can learn how to walk in true victory and stay far away from that nasty ol' Kryptonite!

Give it Some Thought
- Honest assessment: on a scale of 0 to 10, where would you say you are overall in your walk with God?

No walk   *Intimate Walk*
0   1   2   3   4   5   6   7   8   9   10

- Why did you rank yourself that way?

- This may (or may not) be the toughest question for you to answer in this entire study—simply because it requires you to put a name to your sin(s). What is your Kryptonite? What sin(s) keep getting in the way of you growing in your walk with God?

- Why is that particular sin (or sins) your Kryptonite? Why is it so easy to give in to it?

Week 6, Day 2

"Dateline: Egypt, Genesis 8. This is Ammon Ra reporting for station WEGPT, standing here on the banks of what used to be the beautiful Nile.

"The nation of Egypt is still trying to recover from a plague of Biblical proportion that occurred seven days ago.[1] The Hebrew rebel Moses and his detestable brother Aaron have claimed that their God is responsible for the deplorable condition of the water across the land.[2] As of this report, although efforts are underway to dig deep underground,[3] no sources of fresh water can be found anywhere. The wells are filled with blood, as is the Nile and all its tributaries. This has of course had serious repercussions on our grocery stores as all produce, meat and dairy products have been impacted due to a lack of clean water. Although the stench resulting from blood and rotting fish has become unbearable,[4] Pharaoh's administration assures us that all will be back to normal soon.

"This just out! A new plague seems to have been unleashed upon our glorious nation. Just moments ago the two Hebrew insurgents known as Moses and Aaron were seen once again standing by the Nile, arms outstretched over the water, calling upon their God. Suddenly an incalculable mass of frogs erupted from its waters.[5] This station, along with all of our affiliates, is being inundated with reports of similar occurrences happening nationwide. As you can see from these live shots on your screen, the frogs have begun to literally cover the land. Everywhere you look, as far as the eye can see, there is nothing but a heaving mass of frogs.

"Wait just a moment, please ... Unbelievable! Osiris, pan your camera to the left. Ladies and Gentlemen, as you can see, Pharaoh is giving some sort of instructions to his Magi. Now they are approaching the edge of the Nile. Yes, yes, it looks like they are going to perform some type of ritual. Something is happening. I can see movement on the banks. Osiris, can you zoom in? Oh no! There is now another wave—no, wait a moment, not another wave but a whole new *invasion* of frogs. I don't know if you can see this on your screen; I wouldn't have thought this possible, but there are frogs climbing on top of the frogs already here and they continue to move inland. By Ramses, I can't believe my eyes! Folks, we now have a blanket of frogs on top of a blanket of frogs![6]

"I don't know if you can hear me at the station; I can barely hear myself over the insufferable noise these frogs are making, but we have to get to higher ground. This is Ammon Ra reporting on the banks of the desecrated Nile for WEGPT."

A little later, back in the palace, Pharaoh was in a foul mood. Sitting on his throne, he stared at the frog-covered floor. His servants hurried around, futilely trying to remove the frogs from the throne room. Barely hearing the announcement that Moses and Aaron had arrived over the sounds of constant croaking, Pharaoh straightened, attempting to look as regal as he could. With frogs sitting on his lap, his shoulders, and even a large one nestled inside the crown on top of his head, he watched his nemesis walk into the room.

Slowly Moses made his way toward the throne, gently nudging frogs out of the way with the end of his staff, until finally he stood silently before Pharaoh. For agonizing moments they stared at each other, a contest of wills flashing between their eyes. All that could be heard in the throne room was the incessant croaking of the frogs. Finally, Pharaoh spoke.

"Alright, Moses, you win. I can't fight you on this one. Go, ask your God to take the frogs away from me and my people, and I will let your people go to offer sacrifices to your God."

As Moses stood before Pharaoh, he couldn't stop the smile from creeping across his face. Finally, the Israelites could be free from this tyrant and would be allowed to leave Egypt to go serve Elohim! Clearing his throat, Moses bowed his head before Pharaoh in acknowledgement of his offer, then said, "I am so glad to hear you admit that only God has the power and ability to get rid of these frogs. I leave you the honor of setting the time for me to pray for you and your officials and your people, that you and your houses may be rid of the frogs. When, Oh Pharaoh, when would you like God to remove these frogs from your life?"[7]

Galatians 5:1

"For freedom Christ has set us free; stand firm therefore, and do not submit again to a yoke of slavery."

There was a brief pause as Pharaoh thought through how he was going to answer. His response sent a wave of shock throughout the room. "Tomorrow! Ask God to remove the frogs tomorrow."[8] Recognizing that his answer surprised his guests, he continued: "Oh, don't misunderstand me, Moses. I know the situation here is bad. These frogs are unclean, they're unhealthy, they're noisy and you wouldn't believe the amount of complaints that have come into our administration over the last few hours. However, I want one more night with these frogs in my life. We'll let God deal with the frogs tomorrow!"

Don't judge Pharaoh too hastily, my friend. Why not? Because you and I can be just as guilty as he. You see, we all have frogs in our life. Each of us encounters Frequently Recurring Obstacles to Growing Spiritually (F.R.O.G.S.). We all have things that are getting in the way of our walk with God; our own Kryptonite.

Each us has sin issues in our life that are affecting not only us, but everyone around us. There are things we want to hold on to, things we refuse to let go of—even though we know they are making us, and everyone around us, miserable.

Yesterday you wrote down your Kryptonite. That list represents the FROGS in your life. Those are the frequently recurring obstacles that are preventing you from growing spiritually. I want you to take a look at that list. Seriously, take a look at that list right now.

Didn't do the exercise yesterday? Don't have a list yet? Then in the space below, write down the FROGS that are in your life. What sin(s) do you know you need to deal with? You know you need to get rid of them. You know they are hindering your relationship with God, but you keep holding on to them till tomorrow. Go ahead, write them down—I'll wait for you.

- What are the FROGS in your life? What are the sins you know you need to get rid of, but are holding on to for one more night?

Now, look at your list. We need our FROGS to stare us in the face with all of their warts and ugliness. As you look at your list, think about this:

- What is so special about *those* FROGS that you are willing to put them in the place of God in your life?

- What are *they* doing for you that God cannot do?

- Why are you so willing to sacrifice a closer walk with God, just so you can have one more night with *those* FROGS?

- Why are you choosing to wait until tomorrow to get rid of your FROGS?

In Genesis 35, Jacob gathers his whole household together and instructs them to put away the foreign gods they have been worshiping (the FROGS in their life) and purify themselves.[9] What FROGS are you worshipping? What foreign gods are you holding on to in hopes that they will bless you with pleasure, happiness, or whatever else you may be seeking? And why, *why* on God's green earth do you believe that a little "g" god can give you those things, let alone that it even cares about you?

In Exodus 20:3 God makes it abundantly clear that we are to have no other gods before Him. We are to fear the Lord our God and serve Him only. We must never follow after other gods, no matter what they may promise to give us.[10] Guys, whatever is in your life today that has been taking the place of God—get rid of it NOW!

> ## 1 Samuel 7:3
> *"If you are returning to the Lord with all your hearts, then rid yourselves of the foreign gods ... and commit yourselves to the Lord and serve him only, and he will deliver you."*

Week 6, Day 3

Dave was an awesome guy. He had everything going for him. He was at the top of his game. President of a growing company that was really going places; people who not only worked for him, but deeply respected him; a portfolio to die for—he had it all. From his top-floor corner office he could look out on all he had built. He was proud of what he had accomplished, proud of all his employees had done, and proud of his little kingdom.

One day as he was standing at his desk, observing the goings and comings of the people he employed, his assistant, Beth, stepped into the office. "Davey," she said. The quiver in her voice made him spin around to look at her. Tears welled up in her eyes. Rushing over to her, he helped her sit down. "What's wrong, Beth?"

With her head bowed, staring at her fingers she answered, "I'm pregnant. And before you say anything—it's yours, I'm certain." Her announcement hit the floor like a 10-megaton bomb. Dave's heart stopped for a moment, then permanently lodged in his throat. He quickly glanced out the window into the open area beyond his office, wondering if any of his employees heard.

"I haven't said anything to Ryan yet. Oh, Davey, what are we going to do?" Ryan was Beth's husband and one of Dave's top salesmen. The young couple had been married nearly three years. Unfortunately, Ryan wasn't able to make it to the company Christmas party last month, so Dave took it upon himself to make sure Beth enjoyed the evening. Instead of going home as he had originally intended, Dave hung around to help Beth clean up after the party was over. One thing led to another and, well, here they were in a horrible predicament.

Panic seized Dave's chest like an iron fist. What were they going to do? This was a mess—a big mess. No, this wasn't just a mess, it was a catastrophe. This could ruin him in a heartbeat. Everything he had worked so hard to build suddenly felt like a house of cards, ready to collapse around him at the slightest breath.

Ryan was the problem here, Davey was certain. Somehow, he had to get the husband out of the picture so he could take care of Beth properly. But how? Suddenly he had an idea, an absolutely, horrifically good idea: an accident. He would arrange for Ryan to be involved in some type of fatal accident. Once Ryan was out of the picture, Dave would swoop in as the hero, taking Beth as his wife so he could care for the grieving widow and the baby she and Ryan were expecting.

Decision + Deception = Destruction

Does the story sound familiar? Change the environment a bit and you have the account of 2 Samuel 11. It's the miserable story of David, Bathsheba and Uriah. Why did David do such horrible things? What was he thinking?

Actually, that is a very important question to consider. What was he thinking?

I once heard someone say, "You can choose your actions, but you cannot choose the consequences." True statement. Just look at the choices David made.

- He chose to stay home from the war instead of doing his duty as king and leading his men into battle.
- He chose to look at Bathsheba bathing instead of walking away the moment he saw her naked.
- He chose to have sex with a married woman instead of honoring the sanctity of marriage that God had established.
- He chose to lie and deceive by bribing Uriah, encouraging him to sleep with his wife.
- He then chose to murder Uriah instead of obeying the eighth commandment (see Exodus 20:13).

Every bad choice he made just led to another bad choice, and then another, followed by another. Every bad choice led to very bad consequences.

- What were the consequences of David's choices? (See 2 Samuel 11:1 – 12-22.)

Yes, you can choose your actions. Yes, there are consequences to those actions. However, I want you to think about this: You CAN choose your consequences! *"But wait a minute! I thought you just said I can't—make up your mind!"* You read that correctly. You can indeed choose your consequences—by choosing your actions. For example, I can choose to not lose my fingers by choosing to not put my hand under a running lawnmower.

- What choices could David have made that would have changed the consequences?

Before we close out the day, please read the verses listed in the table below. Using the columns to the right of the verses, write out the choice and the consequence.

Verse	Choice	Consequence
Deut. 28:1-8		
Jer. 17:5-8		

These are just a couple of examples. Can you find more? They're sprinkled all throughout Scripture. Choices have consequences. Want good consequences? Make good choices!

Give it Some Thought
- In the story of David and Bathsheba, what was David's Kryptonite?

- Why do we play around with our Kryptonite, our FROGS (sinful habits)?

- Read the following: Proverbs 27:19; Romans 8:5-6, 13:14; and Colossians 3:2. What role does your mind play in temptation and sin?

- Read 2 Corinthians 10:4-5; Romans 12:2; and Philippians 4:8. What can/must we do to change the way we think?

Week 6, Day 4

Jerry paused briefly to wipe the sweat from his forehead. Checking his watch, he realized he'd been digging for over seven hours. Thrusting the worn shovel into the ground, he stepped back to look at his handiwork. Not bad, even if he said so himself. Seven hours of back-breaking work and he had a hole about six feet wide and almost four feet deep. Not nearly deep enough, but still a good day's work considering all the stone he had to move. Grabbing the shovel once again, he heard the sound of someone clearing his throat.

Glancing up, he saw the silhouette of his friend, Eric, standing at the edge of the hole looking down at him. "Jerry, what are you doing?" asked Eric. "I'm digging a cistern!" Jerry replied. "A what?" Smiling up at Eric he repeated, "A cistern. It's an in-ground container for water."

"I know what a cistern is, Jerry. I just don't understand why you're digging it."

111

Jeremiah 2:12-13

"Be appalled, O heavens, at this; be shocked, be utterly desolate, declares the Lord, for my people have committed two evils: they have forsaken me, the fountain of living waters, and hewed out cisterns for themselves, broken cisterns that can hold no water."

"Oh, that's simple! The cistern I dug three weeks ago has gotten a number of cracks in it already, so it's not holding the water anymore." Jerry turned back to the task at hand and begun to dig once again.

"My question still stands, bro. *Why* are you digging a cistern?" Leaning against the shovel handle, Jerry sighed. "Because I need to hold on to the water so we can drink!"

Tossing his hands up in the air, Eric retorted, "Dude! Why don't you just drink from the fresh water gushing out of this huge fountain sitting right here?"

If you read that short story and concluded that Jerry is a foolish man, you would be right. But before we slam down the gavel and pass judgment on him, understand that we are just as guilty.

God has given to us the fountain of living water, Jesus Christ Himself. We have an endless supply of everything we need in Christ.[13] And yet we dig out cisterns that are broken, unable to hold any water. Furthermore, any water they could hold is stagnant and putrid. We create gods (FROGS) that "have mouths, but cannot speak, eyes, but they cannot see; they have ears, but cannot hear, noses, but they cannot smell; they have hands, but cannot feel, feet, but they cannot walk; nor can they utter a sound with their throats" (Psalm 115:4-8).

Guys, it's important that we deal with our broken cisterns, our FROGS, our Kryptonite. Those habitual sins won't provide you with what you're looking for. They may promise you happiness, they may try to guarantee you pleasure, they may tell you that they hold everything you could ever want in life—but they're broken. They won't give you what you need, simply because they cannot. Only Jesus is the answer.

If we are going to live in victory and freedom, it's critical to know exactly what our Kryptonite is doing to us and how we can counter its affects. Why do we respond the way we do when we're around it? Why does it weaken our ability to resist? There is actually a chain reaction of seven things that happen, one right after the other, every time we get near our Kryptonite.

1. As we saw yesterday, it all begins when we are lured by a particular temptation that is especially appealing to us. Somewhere deep inside there is an attraction to it—a lust. This is the most critical piece to the puzzle. Identify and deal with this, and you will avoid the other six steps and be free from the damaging effects of your Kryptonite. The bottom line here is not to give the enemy any ground to stand on.[14]

2. When we give in to the pull of temptation, we will initially make an attempt to resist—after all, that's what a good Christian guy does, right? But that attempt is pathetically insufficient at best. Why? Because we secretly want to experience the pleasure that temptation promises us. Again, if you attack this right here and now you will avoid the trap being set for you. But if your desires and thoughts are not dealt with God's way,[15] that temptation will grow in strength and become much harder to fight.

    *   How do we deal with our thoughts and desires God's way?

3. Because the temptation to give in is growing, our minds begin to come up with excuses as to why it's okay for us to go ahead and sin. We even get to the point where we start validating our choice to give up and give in. Our spiritual vision has been impaired. We are now struggling with "me-opia," seeing things from the perspective of self and how it will benefit King Me.

- What are some excuses we give to validate our choice to sin?

- What's wrong with those excuses?

4. By now our thoughts are almost completely focused on getting the promised pleasure. We begin to truly believe that *"I need this. I have to have this. I must do this."* And we also battle with feelings of defeat and helplessness—*"I just can't get victory over this thing!"* At this point, God is no longer in the picture, or if He is, we have Him pigeonholed into either the box of *"He'll understand and forgive me,"* or *"He's given up on me and I'm on my own."*
   - Why do we push God out of the way?

5. At this point we act out our temptation. We give in and we sin[16]

6. Immediately on the heels of that decision come two totally different emotions, almost simultaneously. First we have the payoff, that brief but powerful moment of temporary pleasure or sense of relief.[17] We experience the "reward" of giving in. But tugging on the shirttails of that feeling is one of shame and guilt.

7. To soothe those overwhelming feelings of guilt, we cry out to God and "confess" our sin to Him. Too often, though, the act of confession is done mostly out of duty and a desire to feel better about ourselves, instead of one of true repentance.

- What is the sign of genuine confession and repentance?

Guys, we need to break free from this cycle. We need to live each day of our lives in the knowledge that we don't have to give in to our FROGS. We don't have to surrender to our Kryptonite. We don't have to sin![18]

God has given you everything you need to be victorious. Only through God's strength can you win.[19] Only through His Divine power are you able to say "no" to sin and live a life free from your Kryptonite.[20]

Give it Some Thought
- Read John 7:37-39. Why do we dig "cisterns" when we already have the Fountain of Living Water?

Week 6, Day 5

Five-year-old Drew came running into the house with a spot on his arm that was bleeding. His dad took a damp paper towel and cleaned off the blood to reveal a small, open wound. What had been a simple mosquito bite was now a bloody hole. Drew had scratched it so much that he ripped away the skin.

Seizing the opportunity to teach his son a valuable lesson, Dad asked, "Drew, why did you dig at the mosquito bite?" "Because it was itchy," came his reply. "Didn't Mommy tell you to leave it alone?" Drew nodded slowly. "So why did you scratch it?" Trying to keep back the tears welling up in his eyes, Drew whimpered, "Because it felt good."

"Does it feel good now?" Dad asked.

"No."

Pausing for a moment to let that point sink in, Dad looked at his boy, smiled and said, "The more you scratch at it, the more it itches. The more you scratch at it, the bigger it gets. The more you scratch at it, the more irritated it becomes and eventually it turns into an open, bleeding wound. So if you didn't want a bleeding sore on your arm, what should you have done?" Without missing a beat, Drew said, "Leave it alone!"

Itchy, Itchy, Itchy
- Why do you sin? Seriously, now, *why* do you sin?

Simply put, we give in to sin because we like its effects. The more you play around with temptation, the more it itches for attention. So you scratch at it and it feels good. The more you play around with temptation, the bigger it gets and the more your flesh wants the forbidden pleasure. So you scratch some more, and it feels good.

Eventually, scratch the itch long enough and hard enough and you will sin. You will create a spiritual wound that hurts. The solution to not irritating that spiritual mosquito bite is to stop scratching the itch.

Give it Some Thought

- How does a Super Man of God stop scratching the itch to sin?

- Share with the guys at least one takeaway you received this week, and what you plan to do about it.

"No temptation has seized you except what is common to man. And God is faithful; he will not let you be tempted beyond what you can bear. But when you are tempted, he will also provide a way out so that you can stand up under it."
2 Corinthians 10:5

Week 7
Temptation with a Capital "T"

Week 7, Day 1

Peter the Perch was not just any perch; he was a black perch. A week ago he measured 14 inches and weighed in at a whopping three pounds! He was definitely on the fast track to being the most important perch in the lake—or so he thought.

Today was the big day. You see, today Peter was going to venture away from the safety of his family's Lily Pad Farm and go into the dark zone, the deep waters—the place where the big fish played. He was tired of always being "safe." Life awaited him out there in the darkness beyond those boring lily pads. Ignoring the warnings of danger and foolhardiness from his friends, Peter swam away, fully confident in his ability to handle on his own whatever life might throw at him.

So focused was he on proving himself to be a grown-up perch, he hardly noticed how quickly he was leaving the security of the lily pads and the protection of his friends behind. Suddenly, out of the corner of his left eye he saw something strange appear from above. He watched it slowly float down, resting only a few meters away. Curiosity got the better of him and he chose to swim away from his intended destination, just for a moment, just to check it out. Hey, it looked interesting. What harm could there possibly be in a short detour?

As Peter got closer, he noticed that this new, intriguing wonder was moving. That was unexpected. Instinct began to kick in, and he slowed his approach. Cautiously drawing nearer, he slowly swam around and around this strange object. It looked harmless enough. It wasn't trying to hurt him in any way. So he gently bumped it, nudging it ever so slightly. Nothing happened. That was a good sign.

As is the way of fish (since they don't have hands like we do), to discover what this new and strange thing was, Peter opened his mouth and sucked it in, spitting it back out immediately. Now that tasted interesting. The synapses in his tiny little brain were firing rapidly. This was definitely worth exploring a little bit more!

He sucked it in again, letting it sit on his tongue for a moment longer than before. He liked it! But it would be foolish to just take it and run before being totally certain it was safe. So he sucked it in, spit it out. Sucked it in, held it, then spit it out. Nothing happened. What amazing fortune had come his way!

Looking around to see if anyone else was watching, Peter made the split-second decision to suck it in one last time and speed off with his new-found prize before anyone else was the wiser. Poor Peter the perch didn't make it.

> ## James 4:7
> *"Submit yourselves therefore to God. Resist the devil, and he will flee from you."*

No Fishing Allowed

Everyone struggles with temptation; it's just a fact of life. Whether it's fighting the urge to eat that second piece of cake, fudge a little on your tax return, lie to your spouse about where you were and what you were doing, steal a lustful glance at that girl on the beach, or not tell your boss the whole story, temptation to sin is all around us.

Many times, along with the temptation comes the desire to blame someone or something else. "Well," we argue, "if my boss weren't so demanding ..." "If my wife would give me a little bit of slack ..." "If that woman didn't dress so provocatively ..." Our tendency is to feel that we have no option, that God has somehow put us in this situation.

In the book of James, we read:

> "When tempted, no one should say, 'God is tempting me.' For God cannot be tempted by evil, nor does He tempt anyone; but each one is tempted when, by his own evil desire, he is dragged away and enticed. Then, after desire has conceived, it gives birth to sin; and sin, when it is full-grown, gives birth to death." James 1:13-15

Focus for a moment on the words "dragged away."

- What comes to your mind when you see those words?

When I think of someone being dragged away, I get the impression that they're being kidnapped—taken, kicking and screaming, against their will. But that is not what this phrase means here. James is not describing something that happens to you while you are unaware or powerless to stop it. This doesn't happen against your will.

- Why do we sometimes feel like we "have no choice" but to sin?

James uses a fishing term that refers to being lured away from a place of safety. Just as the fisherman used a specific lure to capture Peter the Perch, so Satan lures us away from the path God wants us to take. So, what is the lure that draws us? James says it's our own evil desires.

In other words, there is a lust or craving that you have for a particular type of sinful pleasure, and you allow yourself to think about how to satisfy it. It begins as a tickle in the back of your mind. You think about it, considering it, weighing out the pros and cons of such a decision—the risks vs. the temporary pleasure it promises.

Then, as that thought becomes stronger, it creates within you an intense desire to put that thought into action. Like Peter the Perch, you cautiously play around with it for a while. When nothing "bad" happens, you selfishly suck it in and try to speed off without getting caught.

When you do, WHAM!

Give it Some Thought

- Read James 1:14. Why do we fool around with sin? Why do we allow our minds to think about it? Why do we let it divert our attention away from our relationship with God?

- Notice the word "entice" in that verse. What does it mean to be enticed by sin?

- Read Romans 12:1-2; Philippians 4:8; and 2 Corinthians 10:5. What role does *your* mind play in this fishing lure scenario?

- Read James 1:21; 2 Timothy 2:22; 1 Corinthians 10:14; 1 Timothy 6:11; Proverbs 1:15; and 1 Peter 2:11. How can you avoid getting caught by your sin?

Week 7, Day 2

In a couple weeks we'll talk about archenemies, focusing specifically on our archenemy and how he wants to take us down. Not just "us," but YOU! The fact is, our battle isn't with each other (see Ephesians 6:12). Oh, that's what our enemy wants us to think. It gets the attention off of him and what he's doing. It frees him up to do all sorts of nasty things while we are distracted by unimportant matters.

No, our battle is against the evil of Hell itself.[1] Satan is a master at deception. Just ask Eve. Just ask Judas. Just ask David, or Peter, or even me. His ultimate goal is to lead your thinking away from God. His purpose is to turn you against your Heavenly Father, and he knows the best way to do that is to weasel his way into your mind. What you think determines what you do.[2]

This is War!
We are at war, guys. Make no mistake about it. The battles we are engaged in make World War I and II combined look like a child's game. At times this war can seem overwhelming. Am I right? At times it feels like it's never going to let up, never going to end. At times we can feel like we just want to quit.

> # Deuteronomy 31:6
> *"Be strong and courageous. Do not fear or be in dread ... for it is the Lord your God who goes with you. He will not leave you or forsake you."*

Listen to what God says: "When you go out to war against your enemies, and see horses and chariots and an army larger than your own, you shall not be afraid of them, for the Lord your God is with you" (Deuteronomy 20:1). Guys, as a Christian man, as a Super Man of God, you have been delivered out of the very pit of hell itself. You have been adopted into the family of the King of Kings.[3] And as a Prince of the Throne, as a Super Man of God, *you* have been given a crown and an unbelievable inheritance.[4]

Don't ever—ever—let yourself listen to the lies of the enemy that God doesn't care about your battle, that He is going to stand back while you fight the fight of faith and let you flounder and be massacred. That just ain't gonna happen![5]

> ## Romans 8:38-39
> *"Neither death nor life, nor angels nor rulers, nor things present nor things to come, nor powers, nor height nor depth, nor anything else in all creation, will be able to separate us from the love of God in Christ Jesus our Lord."*

That's powerful!

Yes, you will struggle from time to time. Yes, you will experience feelings of discouragement and thoughts like, *"Will I ever be free?"* That's not a bad thing. That's not a sign that you have failed. That's the time you need to get back up out of the mud and muck of life, plant your feet firmly in your faith, draw your sword, face the enemy head on and resist him, shouting, "Bring it, because you shall not pass!"[6]

You *are* Teknon Theos—you *are* a Super Man of God, my friend. You can fight the enemy and win!

Give it Some Thought
- Read Hebrews 12:1. What do you (not the other guy, not the guy who's worse off than you, but YOU) need to do to finish the race well?

- Why is it so important that you "throw off" these sinful weights? Why not just lay them aside?

- This battle will never be easy. In fact, "In your struggle against sin you have not yet resisted to the point of shedding your blood" (Hebrews 12:4). There are many rough times ahead of each of us. Read Colossians 1:13. What does this promise mean to you?

- Read Colossians 1:10-11. In the space below, write out these verses in your own words—make it your prayer to God.

Week 7, Day 3

Nemuel awoke in sheer panic. Bolting out of bed, he threw on his armor as quickly as he could. It was barely dawn. Thick wisps of fog engulfed the camp, making it hard to see. Sounds of organized chaos echoed around him as his friends emerged from their tents, tying their shoes, buckling their belts and positioning their breastplates.

They looked at each other, confused. The blast from the trumpet had rung out—the call to battle, unmistakable. But why? Then he saw it. Rubbing his eyes to be sure he wasn't seeing some apparition, a hand of ice gripped his heart as reality sank in. The rising sun revealed a terrifying sight on top of the ridge—Amalekites!

Finding his regiment and dutifully falling into line, Nemuel tried hard not to throw up the ball of acid that was rapidly forming in the pit of his stomach. *"I'm too young to die,"* he thought. Looking at his brothers-in-arms around him, he knew they were thinking very similar thoughts.

"Gentlemen," shouted Aaron, the Priest. "Today you are drawing near for battle against your enemies: let not your heart faint. Do not fear or panic or be in dread of them, for the Lord your God is he who goes with you to fight for you against your enemies, to give you the victory!"[7]

The Battle Belongs to Whom?

In your battle against sin, have you ever felt like Nemuel? Have you ever felt like tiny little David up against the big and mighty Goliath? Take a moment and read 1 Samuel 17:40-54. Seriously, pause right now and read it—I'll wait.

Now consider this: has God changed? Is the Almighty, All-Supreme, Ever-Eternal and Unchangeable God of the Universe any different today than he was back in Nemuel's day, or in David's time? The God who was with David in that epic battle against Goliath is the same God who is with you right here, right now.[8] The same power He gave to David to defeat that giant in his life, He makes available to you to combat the giant in yours.[9]

In the story of Superman, his powers come from Earth's yellow sun. In real life, your ability to stand firm and resist your archenemy comes from God. God has promised to give you everything you need to fight this battle.[10] Victory isn't something you have to manufacture. Hey, dude, you've tried that in the past and failed miserably, right? That's why you end up feeling so discouraged and defeated. You picked up the sword and tried swinging it at the enemy in your own strength, and missed.

When you and I try to take on the enemy in our own power, we will lose every time—guaranteed. Search your Bible from cover to cover, my friend. You won't find one single verse anywhere that says, "You are from great stock, for greater are you than he that is in the world." Nope. What you *will* find are these words: "You are from God and have overcome (your enemy), for he who is in you is greater than he who is in the world" (1 John 4:4).

Floats Like a Butterfly but Stings Like a Bee

I can vividly remember, as a five-year-old boy, being terrified because I had wandered too close to a bee's nest. They were quite unhappy about my presence and began actively buzzing around my head, way too close for my comfort. I stood there, literally frozen in fear.

Then I heard my dad's voice saying softly, "Son, it's going to be alright. Look at me." Too scared to open my eyes, I whimpered, "No."

"Son," his voice a bit firmer, "look—at—me." Slowly, I opened my eyes to see my father standing just a few feet away. He smiled as he held out his hands and said, "Now, slowly walk toward me."

Once again I squeezed my eyes shut and began shaking uncontrollably. "I, I can't," I stammered.

"Do you trust me?" I heard him ask. I nodded my head. "Then look at me, and start walking toward me."

Terrified of the impending doom I was certain was about to happen, I took a tentative step toward my father, never taking my eyes off him. Surprisingly, nothing happened. The bees didn't go ballistic and dive-bomb me, plastering me with their poisonous stingers; so I took another step. And then another. Again and again I inched my way forward, until I was wrapped in my father's loving embrace.

As I think back on that event, I am reminded of Psalm 118:12-13. There David writes, "They surrounded me like bees; they went out like a fire among thorns; in the name of the Lord I cut them off! I was pushed hard, so that I was falling, but the Lord helped me." Can you relate? Would you say that at times the temptations to sin surround you like bees and poke you like fiery thorns? Have you ever felt like the enemy was pushing you so hard that you were falling? God is there to help you, and through His strength you can cut them off!

Give it Some Thought
- Take some time here and read the following verses. In the space below, write down what stands out to you and why.
  - 2 Samuel 22:1-4, 40

127

- Joshua 1:9

- Psalm 44:5

- Deuteronomy 28:7

- 2 Chronicles 32:7-8

- 2 Kings 6:15-17

- Psalm 138:3

- Isaiah 40:31

- Isaiah 41:10

- Isaiah 54:17

- Luke 1:37

- Romans 8:37-39

- Ephesians 6:10-13

Week 7, Day 4

Satan wants nothing more than for you to stay defeated—even though you have already won the victory through Christ. Your archenemy wants you to believe you're no Super Man. He wants you to live in the false belief that you cannot win the war. Think about when he tempted Christ in the wilderness.[11] How did Jesus defeat each and every temptation the enemy threw at him? He used Scripture!

So, let's put all of our focus today on what God has to say about living in victory. Below, you will find some verses followed by empty space after each one. Read the verse, then jot your personal thoughts about what that verse is saying and how you can apply it to your life.

- "Our God is a God of salvation, and to God, the Lord, belong deliverances from death." (Psalm 68:20)

- God stands ready to "Deliver (your) soul from death, yes, (your) feet from falling." Why? "That (you) may walk before God in the light of life." (Psalm 56:13)

- "Say of the Lord, 'He is my refuge and my fortress, my God, in whom I trust." (Psalm 91:2)

- "You are a hiding place for me; you preserve me from trouble; you surround me with shouts of deliverance." (Psalm 32:7)

- "The Lord will rescue me from every evil deed and bring me safely into his heavenly kingdom. To him be the glory for ever and ever. Amen" 2 Timothy 4:18.

- "The Lord is my rock and my fortress and my deliverer, my God, my rock, in whom I take refuge, my shield, and the horn of my salvation, my stronghold" Psalm 18:2.

- "As for me, I am poor and needy, but the Lord takes thought for me. You are my help and my deliverer; do not delay, O my God" Psalm 40:17.

Let's close out today with this promise: "Call upon me in the day of trouble; I will deliver you, and you shall glorify me." (Psalm 50:15)

Week 7, Day 5

In the space below, answer this question: What is a "conqueror"?

Now, please read Romans 8:37.

Don't you just love the expression, *"more* than conquerors"? It's filled with so much power and encouragement. It's a phrase that means we haven't just won a battle ... we've won the war! It speaks of being an *over*-conqueror, winning the war with success to spare, ending up supremely victorious. In short, being a Super Man! Is that awesome, or what?

Why, then, do we struggle with feelings of defeat and discouragement? Why do we feel *less* than a conqueror when we've given in (for the umpteenth time) to our temptation?

Could it be that we don't yet fully understand what it means to be more than a conqueror? What is required of us to win the war with "success to spare"?

1. Understand this: you cannot win the war on your own. Read Romans 8:37 again. We are more than conquerors only through the power Christ gives us.[12] He gives us that power[13] not because of any great and glorious thing we have done, or are capable of doing, but simply because of His amazing love, mercy, and grace toward us.

Think about that for a moment. In fact, if you need to, re-read the point above. You and I will win the war against our archenemy because "(we) are from God and have overcome ... for he who is in (us) is greater than he who is in the world" (1 John 4:4).

On my own, I will fail. But I'm not on my own and neither are you. "What then shall we say to these things? If God is for us, who can be against us?" (Romans 8:31). It's "according to the riches of his glory" that God strengthens you "with power through his Spirit in your inner being" (Ephesians 3:16).

2. Believe this: God has a plan for your life. "All things work together for good" (Romans 8:28). Do you believe that? Don't give me the "Sunday School answer" here. Be real. Be raw. Be honest. Do you believe, truly believe in the deepest core of your being, that "it is God who works in you"?[14]

Never forget that God—only God—"is able to do far more abundantly than all that we ask or think, according to the power at work within us" (Ephesians 3:20).

3. Do this: pray! Invest time on your knees talking with your Heavenly Father. Tell Him your frustrations, your fears, and admit your failures. Cry out to Him from your broken heart.

To know victory, talk to the Victor! To be able to overcome, invest time with the Overcomer!

Give it Some Thought
- Read James 4:7. What are the two things you must do to be victorious?

- What does it mean to submit to God?

- What does it mean to resist the Devil?

- Share with the guys at least one takeaway you received this week, and what you plan to do about it.

"Set your minds on things above, not on earthly things."
Colossians 3:2

Week 8
The Fall of a Super Man of God

Week 8, Day 1

The sun was beginning to rise above the horizon as Abraham and Lot stood on top of a hill, talking about the many ways God had blessed them. From their vantage point they could see all of their flocks and herds as well as the hundreds of tents belonging to their servants dotting the countryside. God had indeed blessed them.

Soon their discussion was interrupted by a disturbingly intense commotion. Coming up the hillside were the sounds of their herdsmen bickering, yet again, about whose sheep belonged to whom and whose grass they were grazing on. Abraham and Lot stood there, watching the foremen attempt to stop the fight. Abraham leaned heavily on his staff and began shaking his head. Pursing his lips, he let out a big sigh and turned to his nephew. "Lot," he said, "we have to do something about this. This quarreling between our herdsmen just cannot go on any longer."

"I agree, Uncle, but what do you suggest?" Lot replied. Abraham looked heavenward and prayed for wisdom. After a few moments of silence, he had an idea, a brilliant idea. "Look around, Nephew. Look at all the land before us that God has given us. Here's what I suggest. Let's part company. If you want to go east, I'll go west. Or, if you choose to go west, I'll go east. It doesn't really matter to me, so I'll let you decide."

Lot always knew there was something he liked about his uncle. Leaning forward, he looked to the west and wrinkled his nose.

Nothing very promising in that direction. Turning to the right, he looked east. Now there was some prime land! The whole plain of the Jordan was lush and green. The sun glinted off the streams that watered the plain. There was even a booming metropolis off in the distance—a great place to do business.

"Uncle," Lot said, "since you are giving me first dibs, I choose to go east!"[1]

Me First

Scripture tells us that "Lot chose *for himself* the whole plain of the Jordan" (Genesis 13:11, emphasis mine). Never forget that we always do what we do because in our hearts we want what we want. Our actions will always follow the intentions of our heart. Because Lot's heart was all about self, he chose—*for himself*—to go east and leave his uncle with what Lot thought was second best.

As we will see shortly, that choice led to other choices which in turn led to other choices—all of which resulted in the fall of a Super Man of God. "Wait a minute," you say. "Lot? Are you calling Lot a Super Man of God?" No, I'm not—but God is.

If you're familiar with the story of Sodom and Gomorrah,[2] you will recall that God "condemned the cities of Sodom and Gomorrah by burning them to ashes, and made them an example of what is going to happen to the ungodly." Before destroying those cities for their wickedness, God sent two of his angels and "rescued Lot, a righteous man, who was distressed by the filthy lives of lawless men (for that righteous man, living among them day after day, was tormented in his righteous soul by the lawless deeds he saw and heard)" (2 Peter 2:6-8).

Three times in just two verses God calls Lot a *righteous man*. Just so we're clear, the word "righteous" means exactly what you would expect it to mean in the Bible. It refers to a person who stands approved and accepted by God.

Guys, we need to understand that Lot was a righteous man before God. He stood before God as one approved and accepted. So, that begs the question, what is it exactly that makes a guy "righteous" in God's eyes? Because when you look at the life of Lot in Scripture, we see nothing to indicate he was a righteous man. What makes a person righteous before God?

- "By *faith* (Abel) was commended a righteous man." (Hebrews 11:4)
- "Abram *believed* the Lord, and (God) credited it to him as righteousness." (Genesis 15:6)
- "Clearly no one is justified before God by the law, because 'the righteous will live by *faith*.'" (Galatians 3:11)
- "No one will be declared righteous in his sight by observing the law … this righteousness from God comes *through faith* in Jesus Christ to all who believe." (Romans 3:20, 22)

Galatians 5:17

"For the desires of the flesh are against the Spirit, and the desires of the Spirit are against the flesh, for these are opposed to each other, to keep you from doing the things you want to do."

Think carefully about what you just read. God makes it abundantly clear that no one can stand before Him as one approved and accepted based upon their good deeds. No one stands before God approved and accepted based on the merits of his obedience to His Holy Law. The single requirement for being a righteous man is putting your faith in God.

So here is a very important question for you to consider. In fact, it is arguably the most important question you will ever be asked in your lifetime. If you were to die right now, where would you spend eternity?

Okay, what does that have to do with Lot being a Super Man of God? For that matter, what does that question have to do with you or me being a Super Man of God? Faith in Christ alone for your salvation, believing with all your heart that Jesus paid the penalty for your sin in full; accepting the gift of eternal life that only Christ can give places you in a right standing before God. If you have done that, you are a righteous man. You are Teknon Theos—son of God.

Paul told the Philippian jailer that all he had to do was put his faith in Christ and he would be saved.³ Through faith we become a part of God's family. Have *you* done that? You see, it's by God's grace that you are saved. Salvation is only through the act of believing in what Christ did on the Cross of Calvary as opposed to what you can do to save yourself.⁴ So again I ask, have you done that?

If your answer is yes, if you have put your faith and trust in Christ alone for your salvation and eternal destiny, then you are considered by God to be a righteous man. You are a Super Man of God. Let me quickly add here, if you have never put your faith in Jesus Christ, if you don't know what I'm talking about, visit our website, grab my phone number and give me a call. I would love to talk with you.

Lot was a righteous man. Lot was Teknon Theos. Lot was a Super Man of God. No, he didn't act like it. He certainly didn't live like it. But he was. And because he was, he was also a very miserable man. The sinful choices he made, and the wicked lifestyle he was living, conflicted with his righteous soul.⁵

What about you? As we just saw, if you're a born-again believer you are a righteous man. You are a Super Man of God. Are you acting like it? Are you living like it? Or are you experiencing conflict within your righteous soul?

Give it Some Thought
- Read Galatians 5:17; Roman 7:18, 21-25 and 8:5-6, 13. Why is there such a conflict between the flesh and the Spirit?

- Read Song of Solomon 2:15. In what ways are you letting little foxes (little compromises) into your life?

- What were Lot's choices and the resulting consequences in his life?

Week 8, Day 2

Superman never knowingly chooses to walk into a room filled with Kryptonite, but we often do. The choices we make have consequences.

Action – Consequence: the Choice is Yours

Peter tells us that as a righteous man, Lot was "greatly distressed by the sensual conduct of wicked men" (2 Peter 2:7). In other words, Lot was fighting an intense spiritual battle. On the one hand, as a righteous man, he wanted to please God. On the other hand, as a self-centered man, he wanted to please King Me. As Paul describes in Galatians 5:17, his flesh was in conflict with the Spirit, and the Spirit was in conflict with his flesh. They were two polar opposites locked in fierce warfare. Lot's story is a serious reminder of what can happen when you allow the flesh and its sinful desires to win out.

On Week 6, Day 3, we learned that we choose our consequences by choosing our actions. Now think about that principle as it relates to Lot (and us). Every choice he made led to a consequence. Choose wrong, pay the price. Make the right choice, enjoy the right consequence.

Lot's problems began with self on the throne of his heart. Lot chose for himself. And because Lot was on the throne, he saw nothing wrong with the choices he was making. So here's a vital question for you— who is sitting on the throne of your heart? What are the things you are choosing *for yourself*?

In fact, God spoke with Cain about this same thing just before Cain chose to murder his brother. He said, "If you do well, will you not be accepted? And if you do not do well, sin is crouching at the door. Its desire is contrary to you, but you must rule over it" (Genesis 4:7). What consequences do you want? The choice is yours.

A Super Man of God is Always on Guard
Do you remember how Solomon learned the hard way that man's primary purpose in life is to fear God and keep His commandments?[6] Well, I have a question for that wise old sage. "Hey Solomon, what is the most important thing I can do in life so that I will continuously fear God and always keep His commandments?"

James 3:16 (NIV '84)
"For where you have envy and selfish ambition, there you find disorder and every evil practice."

"Above all else," comes Solomon's reply, "guard your heart, for it is the wellspring of life" (Proverbs 4:23 NIV '84). Now there is some great counsel! What a fantastic tidbit of wisdom! The most important thing I can do—the most important thing I *must* do, above all else—is to guard my heart. Nothing, absolutely nothing, is more important than this. Above all else, always post a guard around your heart.

Okay, great. The most important thing I must do is guard my heart; but what exactly is my "heart" and why is it so vital that I guard it? To answer the first part of the question we need to go to the original language of that verse—Hebrew. There we learn that the word "heart" refers to the place where thinking and decision-making occur. In other words, the mind.

Above all else guard your mind. Let me repeat: nothing is more important than placing a guard around your mind. Why? Because out of your mind come the things of life. What you think will eventually be revealed in what you do.[7] You see, "For as he thinks in his heart, so *is* he" (Proverbs 23:7 NKJV). Guard your mind and you guard your life.

Lot failed to guard his heart. He failed to protect his mind. He chose to relax, to let down his spiritual guard and allow the wickedness of the world around him to penetrate and permeate his thinking. As a result, he was in spiritual turmoil and he made very bad choices.[8]

What is the focus of your mind? What thoughts do you entertain? What you think about will influence what you do. Are the daily choices you are making in life for the benefit of self or for the glory of God?

I can't help but wonder, had Lot followed the principle of seeking first the kingdom of God and His righteousness,[9] would his story have had a totally different ending? Lot is long dead and gone, so he cannot go back and change the events of his life. What about you?

Give it Some Thought
- What is the primary function of a guard?

- What qualities and characteristics make up a good guard?

- How do your answers to the above two questions apply to guarding your mind?

Week 8, Day 3

I think it's safe to say that Lot made some really bad choices in life, and he paid very serious consequences as a result. Listen carefully, guys—we can be guilty of making the same mistakes as Lot. Any time we put self on the throne, we are destined for trouble.

With King Me on the throne of his heart, Lot chose to move in with the wicked people of Sodom and Gomorrah. That was a dumb move on his part. Oh, I'm sure it made sense to him at the time. Possibly he saw it as a shrewd business decision. Maybe he even thought he could be a great soul-winner in the process. I don't know what his rationale was, but he made the fateful choice to dwell *with* them. He chose to relax around them and let down his spiritual guard. 1 Corinthians 15:33 warns us to "not be deceived: 'Bad company ruins good morals.'" Lot surrounded himself with bad company, and it corrupted his godly ethics and principles and it ruined his testimony big-time.

- He sat in the gateway of the city (an earned position of authority and respect).[10] How do you think he earned that honor in the midst of such wickedness?

- He called those wicked men his friends and his brothers (a term of endearment).[11] Why do you think he felt free to call them that? Furthermore, why do you think they allowed him to call him that?

- He handed over his virgin daughters to be gang-raped.[12] In what universe would that be considered to be okay? How did he get to the point where he was able to justify that decision in his mind?

- He had no testimony for God within his family.[13] That degraded over a period of time. What do you think he did to lose that testimony?

- Even when the destruction of the city was imminent, he delayed leaving.[14] What possible reason would he have for wanting to hang around?

- His wife looked back longingly to that wicked city and instantly lost her life.[15] What happened to Lot's spiritual leadership and influence in his home?

- His daughters committed incest with him.[16] I'm not even going to touch this one except to say that choices lead to consequences.

How could any of that have happened? How could a righteous man, how could a Super Man of God, fall so far and do something so despicable? It began when he played around with his Kryptonite.

Suppose you had stood on that hillside with Abraham and Lot on the day Lot chose to move east. What if you stopped Lot before answering his uncle, and warned him not to go down there? Had you told him everything that was going to happen—all the self-centered, sinful choices he was going to make and the serious consequences that would follow those choices—he would have looked at you as if you were a purple alien with a single eye in the center of your forehead that was oozing green goo. He would have called you a nutcase. No way would that ever happen to him. Choices—consequences.

Guys, I'm standing on a hillside right now next to you. I'm warning you: stop playing with your Kryptonite. Your self-centered choices will have far-reaching consequences. I know you think you're in control. I know you believe the worst will never happen to you. I also know you're dead wrong. Choices—consequences.

A Super Man of God Knows Where to Pitch His Tent

Lot "pitched his tent toward Sodom" (Genesis 13:12 KJV). He intentionally set up his house so that from the moment he opened the flap of his tent in the morning to the time he closed it at night, he was exposing himself—and his family—to the wickedness of the world around him, day in and day out.

A Super Man of God knows where to pitch his tent. Peter tells us that Lot's righteous soul was in torment every moment of every day he lived in that wicked city. Do you know why? It was because of the wicked things he *saw and heard* every single day.[17] He pitched his tent toward Sodom. He chose for himself to allow sin to enter his thoughts daily. He refused to "take captive every thought to make it obedient to Christ" (2 Corinthians 10:5 NIV '84).

Would you say the world we live in today is any better than Sodom and Gomorrah? That same wickedness surrounds each and every one of us. We are daily exposed to that same core issue. We are surrounded by self-centered, pleasure-oriented, God-denying wickedness. And it is contagious. That is why you must always guard your mind.

What are you allowing into your tent? What are you allowing your eyes to see and ears to hear? What is your mind feeding upon every day? Consider this: what you see and hear impacts what you think, and what you think influences what you do!

Your tent—your mind—must always be a place of purity and godliness at all times. Choices—consequences.

Give it Some Thought

- In what ways are you surrounded by the self-centered, pleasure-oriented, God-denying wickedness of this world?

- What are some ways you can (and should) guard your mind?

Week 8, Day 4

A Super Man of God Always Protects His Eyes

We just learned that a Super Man of God knows where to pitch his tent, and he is always guarding his mind. One of the ways he does this is by being extremely careful about what he allows his eyes to see. Lot's righteous soul was in torment. He experienced intense spiritual warfare daily because he pitched his tent in the wrong direction—he allowed his eyes not just to see the evil of the world around him, but to look on it with approval and appreciation—and it wore him down.

Every day we are faced with choices—choices about what we allow our eyes to see. Those choices have consequences.

When walking around in the pitch black of night, I'm willing to bet that a flashlight would be a very welcome help. How foolish would it be for someone to turn on a flashlight, point it to the right and yet walk to the left? Pretty stupid, right? Wherever that light is pointing is the direction you are going to walk. Why? Because that light is there to show you where to go and what obstacles to avoid.

> # 1 John 2:15-16
> *"Do not love the world or the things in the world. If anyone loves the world, the love of the Father is not in him. For all that is in the world—the desires of the flesh and the desires of the eyes and pride of life—is not from the Father but is from the world."*

In the most famous message Jesus ever preached (known to us as the Sermon on the Mount), He said, "The eye is the lamp of the body. If your eyes are good, your whole body will be full of light. But if your eyes are bad, your whole body will be full of darkness" (Matthew 6:22-23 NIV '84).

Think of a "lamp" as a flashlight. Only instead of the light shining "out" from your eyes (like X-Men's Cyclops), it's actually shining inward. That "light" (what you see) is showing you how to live, where to go and what to do. What happens when the majority of the things we allow our eyes to see each day are sinful and ungodly?

Jesus is telling us that the things we see have a powerful influence on the things we do. If our eyes are good, if they are focused on things that will glorify God, then our actions and behavior will also glorify Him. However, if we allow our eyes to continuously view things that are ungodly, those things will wear us down and our lifestyle will eventually reflect that choice. Choices—consequences.

Daily we need to make decisions about what we will read, watch and even what we will listen to.[18] Wouldn't it be great if God regularly published *The Throne Room's Weekly Review: Heaven's TV and Movie Guide* to show us which things received His two-thumbs-up? Well, in a sense He has. No, you won't find where God says, "Thou shalt watch these things and thou shalt not watch those;" but as you daily invest time in studying God's Word, you will be able to quickly identify those things that are going to help you grow spiritually and those that can draw you away from God.

So how do I know what I should look at and what I should not? Certainly, there are some things that are fairly obvious, like pornography—a definite no-no.[19] But what about those things that fit into those undefined, grey areas? Look to Scripture. Seriously, dude—turn to the Word!

- "(God's) word is a lamp to my feet and a light to my path." (Psalm 119:105)
- "The unfolding of (God's) words gives light." (Psalm 119:130)
- God's "commandment is a lamp and (His) teaching a light." (Proverbs 6:23)
- "The commandment of the Lord is pure, enlightening the eyes." (Psalm 19:8)
- God's Word is "a lamp shining in a dark place." (2 Peter 1:19)

> ## Psalm 25:15 (NIV '84)
> *"My eyes are ever on the Lord, for only He will release my feet from the snare."*

In Philippians 4:8 we are instructed to keep our *minds* focused on things that are true, noble, right, pure, lovely and admirable. Since what we see has a direct impact on what we think, doesn't it stand to reason that the things we see should also be true, noble, right, pure, lovely and admirable? In the final analysis, anything you see that takes your love and focus away from God, from His Word, and from doing His will, doesn't belong in your life. Choices—consequences.

In Everything Turn, Turn, Turn

I love the challenge from David to turn our eyes away from looking at worthless things.[20] That's solid advice. In fact, he goes on to warn us to always be careful about what we set before our eyes.[21] When we allow the wickedness of this world to enter our eyes and penetrate our minds, we run the high risk of our thought patterns becoming altered, which will eventually impact our behavior. What you think will affect what you do.

So, what do you watch on TV? What movies do you watch? What music do you listen to? What online games do you play? What magazines do you read?

"Oh, but Steve, it's just harmless entertainment!" you say. "I'm able to discern the difference between what's happening on screen and real life. No harm, no foul." Really? Let me challenge you to carefully consider what you are allowing to enter the flaps of your tent. What ungodly things are you exposing your mind to? What seed thoughts might the enemy be planting? Seeds grow. What crop will those seeds produce? Maybe not right away, but over time those seeds will sprout into weeds that will choke out the Word.[22]

I know, I'm really meddling here. For some of you I just became a crazy lunatic who's thumping Scripture at you—but hear me out. If you do not guard your heart by being careful of what you allow your eyes to see, the deception of Satan will slowly creep in and warp your thinking, pulling you away from God.

Never forget that bad company corrupts good morals. What kind of company are you allowing into your home and into your mind by way of your eyes? If you allow your eyes to see that which does not glorify God, you are allowing your mind to think on things that do not glorify God. Unless you guard your mind, it can result in a life that will not glorify God. Choices—consequences.

Give it Some Thought

- Read Psalm 101:7. How can this verse apply to the things you watch on TV and in movies?

- Read 1 Thessalonians 5:21-22; Romans 16:17; and Mark 12:30. How can these verses be a litmus test to help you determine what you should see and what you should not?

Week 8, Day 5

Guarding the Gates

This week we've focused on one powerful truth: your eyes and your ears are gateways into your mind. What you allow to enter through those gates will impact your effectiveness for Christ.

> What we see/hear impacts what we think;
> What we think influences what we do!

That's why, above all else, we are to guard our minds at all times. Logically, if I am going to effectively guard my mind, I must also guard my eyes and ears as well.

We are commanded in Scripture to fix our gaze on that which is directly in front of us—our eyes should always be looking straight ahead.[23] Why? Because that is where God is. Because that is the direction God's will is leading you. When your eyes are locked on to God[24] you cannot—you will not—go wrong.

Gentlemen, it is vital to your spiritual growth that you always set your focus on God. Never let it wander from Him, no matter what lure the enemy may be using in an attempt to draw your attention. Always be focused. Always be strong. Be God's man of steel. Don't play around with your Kryptonite. Don't even think about it. Don't allow the worldly things you see each day to turn you away from following Christ.[25]

Remember, what we see influences what we think; and what we think impacts what we do. That is why ...
- We are to fix our eyes on Jesus. (Hebrews 12:2)
- We are to fix God's words in our minds and in our hearts. (Deuteronomy 11:18)
- We are to fix our eyes, not on what is seen, but on what is unseen. (2 Corinthians 4:18)
- We are to fix our thoughts on Christ. (Hebrews 3:1)

What you allow yourself to think about—everything that goes on in your mind—matters to God. Scripture is quite clear on the issue. Set a guard around your mind, my friend. Lock it down tightly by being very careful about what you see and what you hear.

The King's Finger Moved

Jesha was a servant, second-tier, in the palace of the King. He had worked hard to move up the ranks and was proud of his position. As a 2-T servant, he was privileged to be stationed in the throne room. Although his job wasn't easy, it was quite simple. Every day he would sit on a hewn block of wood, 25 feet off to the left side of the throne. Anytime the King needed him, His Majesty would make a simple gesture with his finger. Immediately Jesha would be at his side to do whatever task was assigned to him.

Most of the time he was constantly on the move. Running to the kitchen to get a cup of pomegranate juice. Going to the library to bring back a specific scroll. Taking an honored guest to his room for the night. Whatever the King needed, Jesha was there.

However, there were times when all he did was sit for hours on end and stare at the King's left hand. He dare not look away, ever. His job was that important. He could not afford to take his eyes off the King. To look away, to allow his attention to be taken from his Master for even a brief moment, could be disastrous. Choices—consequences.

> ## Psalm 123:1-2
> *"To you I lift up my eyes, O you who are enthroned in the heavens! Behold, as the eyes of servants look to the hand of their master, so our eyes look to the Lord our God."*

Where are your eyes focused? Are they turned inward toward King Me, or are they focused and fixed on the King of Kings?

Give it Some Thought

- What are some ways we can keep our eyes focused and fixed on Christ?

- What are some ways we can guard the gates of our eyes and ears?

- Share with the guys at least one takeaway you received this week, and what you plan to do about it.

"Get behind me, Satan! You are a hindrance to me.
For you are not setting your mind on the things of God,
but on the things of man."
Matthew 16:23

Week 9
The Archenemy of a Super Man of God

Week 9, Day 1

Let's start off with a quiz. In the table below you will see a listing of superheroes on the left and their archenemies on the right. Draw a line connecting each superhero with his specific nemesis.

Superhero	Archenemy
Batman	Lex Luthor
Superman	Magneto
Thor	Red Skull
Professor X	Joker
Captain America	Green Goblin
Wolverine	Loki
Spiderman	Sabretooth
The Fantastic Four	Doctor Doom

So, how did you do? Don't worry if you struggled with it, or even failed miserably. The point here is not how well you are able to identify the archenemy of a fictitious superhero.[1] Rather, as a Super Man of God, how well can you identify *your* archenemy? Don't freak out here, but yes—you do have an archenemy.

If you're anything like me, a definition is probably in order here. What exactly is an archenemy? How is that different from a regular enemy? Inquiring minds want to know! Actually, a Super Man of God *needs* to know. You see, an archenemy is someone who is extremely hostile and opposed to a specific person. An archenemy hates you and wants nothing more than to see your total annihilation. So, he hounds you. He assaults you. He haunts you day and night. He is relentless in his attacks. He won't quit until you are destroyed.

Hitler: Archenemy to the World
If I were to ask you to tell me about the Battle of the Bulge during World War II, would you be able to describe it to me? Most of us remember the name, but not the details.

It was winter of 1944, and the Allies had finally pushed Germany back behind its borders. The Nazi war machine was falling apart and the continual bombing raids of the Allies were making it so that Hitler's forces would never rise again.

Celebration reigned across Europe. Everyone was rejoicing in Germany's defeat. The war was over. One problem, though: somebody forgot to tell Hitler.

Even as his forces were being crushed and driven back, the Führer was secretly devising a plan for one last glorious offensive. Undiscovered and untouched underground factories whipped out weapons and ammunition, transport vehicles and tanks at an unbelievable rate. Germany's young men and old convicts were drafted and trained for war. As Europe rejoiced, Hitler planned. As the Allies celebrated, Hitler attacked. The result: Thousands of good men died because somebody forgot that the enemy still lived and that the war was not yet over.

Satan: Archenemy to all Christians
In the spiritual world, do you know anybody who fits the description of an archenemy? Do you know of someone who is more spiritually cruel, more evil than Hitler, Stalin, Castro, Mao Tse-Tung, Saddam

Hussein and Bin Laden combined? Can you think of someone who is extremely hostile and opposed to you as a Christian, someone who wants nothing more than to see you destroyed? I'm willing to wager you can. In fact, I'd bet the farm (if I owned one) that you've already experienced his attacks.

- Read Zechariah 3:1; Luke 22:31; Matthew 13:39; John 8:44; Ephesians 4:27, 6:11; and James 4:7. Who is your archenemy?

Here's the problem. We know the war has already been won. Because of Christ's victory on the Cross of Calvary, Satan and his demons have been beaten. So, we're off celebrating while he is still on the offensive. We're sitting back in our spiritual easy chairs while he is practicing guerilla warfare. We've forgotten that the enemy still lives. Yes, the war is over, but the battle is still raging. We must not let down our guard—not for even a moment. The archenemy of your soul is still at large!

Give it Some Thought

- In what ways have you experienced the archenemy attacking you?

- Why does Satan hound you—what is his purpose and goal?

- Read 1 Peter 5:8. How does a lion hunt? When stalking his prey, what is he looking for?

- How does your answer to the above question apply to Satan's strategy with you?

- Read Ephesians 6:11-13; Psalm 119:9, 11; Galatians 5:16 and James 4:7. In what ways can you counter his strategy?

Week 9, Day 2

Rabrialle could barely contain his excitement. As far back as he could remember, this day above all other days was most special to him. This was the day when he and all the other angels were to personally appear before Yahweh. Humans would call this a performance review —appearing before the boss in hopes of getting a raise. How typical. How selfish and self-centered. He preferred to call this his sacrifice of praise.

Around him he could see all his friends, anticipation beaming from their faces. "Next!" The booming voice of Michael the Archangel caught his attention. It suddenly dawned on him that Michael was looking straight at him. His heart skipped a beat. It was his turn.

Just as Rabrialle stepped forward, a loud commotion started behind him. Before he could even turn to look, a larger angel came barreling his way forward, knocking Rabrialle onto the floor. Looking up, he saw the back of Lucifer charging toward the throne! Pulling his sword from its sheath, Rabrialle surged forward. How dare the fallen angel defile the throne room with his filthy presence?

"Hold!" came the cry from the throne. Yahweh's voice, as it echoed through the hall, was unmistakable. Immediately Rabrialle dropped to his knees in obedience.

Silence fell upon the holy chamber as God spoke. "So, Lucifer, where have you come from?" A sneer appeared on Lucifer's face as he replied. "From roaming through the earth, where you banished me. I've covered every square inch of it … but then, you already knew that."

"Ahh," God responded with a smile, "and have you noticed my servant Job? There is no one on earth like him. He has chosen to live a life that is blameless and upright. Now there is a man who fears Me and purposely turns away from anything that is evil."

Lucifer laughed and then spat on the ground. A collective gasp rose from the angels. Rabrialle's hand automatically went back to the hilt of his sword. He could hardly contain himself. But the Creator simply looked at him and shook his head. The message was clear: leave Lucifer alone.

"Does Job fear you for nothing?" Lucifer asked. "C'mon, God. What do you take me for, an idiot? You've put a hedge of protection around him, around his household, and even around his possessions. You've blessed everything his does. No wonder he fears you!" Lucifer paused for a moment. He slowly looked around the throne room at each of the angels, eyes settling on Rabrialle. Again, Rabrialle fought hard to keep himself in check.

"But," Lucifer continued as he turned back toward the Throne, "stretch out your hand against him and strike everything he has, and I guarantee you that he will curse you to your face."

Without even a moment's pause, God responded. "Very well, then, everything he has is in your hands, but on the man himself do not lay a finger." Satisfied, Satan spun around and made his way out of the Throne Room, the angels quickly clearing a path for him. *"Poor Job,"* thought Rabrialle.

When it was time once again to appear before the Throne, Rabrialle had all but forgotten about the events surrounding the last review. As they walked into the Holy Chamber, to everyone's surprise, once again Lucifer was standing before God.

"Well, Lucifer," they heard Yahweh say, "have you considered my servant Job? Even after you destroyed everything he had, there is still no one on earth like him. Even though you cajoled me into allowing you to bring him to ruin without cause, he has maintained his integrity and is still a blameless and upright man who continues to fear me and consistently turns away from doing wrong."

"Eh," Lucifer shrugged. "Skin for skin! A man will gladly give up all he has to save his own life." Satan's eyelids became mere slits as he leaned toward the throne. With index finger pointing directly at God's chest, he lowered his voice to almost a whisper. Rabrialle strained to hear what was being said. "But stretch out your hand and strike his body, and I promise you he will curse you to your face."

"Very well, Lucifer; Job is in your hands." Lucifer grinned as he turned to leave. This was going to be fun. As he began walking off, God's voice boomed throughout the chamber. "However!" A cold chill ran down Lucifer's spine. Refusing to turn toward the throne, he waited to hear what God had to say. "Lucifer, you must spare his life."[2]

I'm sure you know how the story ends. The entire book of Job is worthy of reading. It is an eye-opener to just how evil our archenemy truly is. Not only did Satan attack Job's possessions (including all his children) but also his person—both physically (with boils from head to foot) and emotionally (his wife and closest friends turned on him).

Abaddon the Destroyer – Archenemy of the Soul
The Hebrew name for Satan is Abaddon,[3] which literally means "destruction." *That's* your archenemy. Satan, The Destroyer, is dogging your every step. He's the one who is trying to take you down, just like

he tried to do with Job. He's not just your enemy, he is your archenemy.

Jesus Himself warns us that Satan is here to kill, steal and destroy.[4] That's his goal, but what are his tactics? How do we protect ourselves from his diabolical schemes? A good defense happens when you know your enemy and what he is capable of doing. But can we really know what our archenemy is up to? You bet!

We don't have to be outwitted by Satan, because we are not ignorant of his tactics.[5] Here are just some of the things we know about him:
- He is a crafty deceiver (Genesis 3:1, 13);
- he is the tempter (Matthew 4:3; 1 Thessalonians 3:5);
- he is Beelzebub—ruler of the demons (Matthew 12:24);
- he is a murderer and the father of all lies (John 8:44);
- he is The Evil One (Matthew 6:13; John 17:15);
- he is the god of this age (2 Corinthians 4:4);
- he is the ruler of the kingdom of the air (Ephesians 2:2);
- he disguises himself as an angel of light (2 Corinthians 11:14);
- he is the accuser of God's people (Revelation 12:10);
- and He is the dragon, that ancient serpent (Revelation 12:7-9).

Guys, hear me out. Let me remind you that Satan is still alive and well on planet Earth. He is still that crafty deceiver who is out to destroy you by any means possible. Yes, the war is over, but the battle rages on. Yes, as Super Men of God we live on the victory side, but the archenemy of our souls hasn't quit. He loves to tempt you with his lies and then flood you with guilt and shame after you yield to him. His most effective, most-used weapon in his vast arsenal is deception. Beware, the father of lies is out to deceive you.

Give it Some Thought
- What are some of the most common lies Satan whispers in *your* ear?

- Why does Satan want to take you down?

- Read Ephesians 6:17. What weapon has God given you that is most effective in your battle against your foe?

- How adept are you at using that weapon? What must you do to improve?

Week 9, Day 3

In *Star Wars: Episode VI – Return of The Jedi*[6] Luke Skywalker surrenders himself to the evil Darth Vader in the hopes of saving his father. As Vader leads his son to meet the Emperor, Luke turns to his father and says, "I know there is still good in you; the Emperor hasn't driven it from you fully. That is why you couldn't destroy me."

Later in the movie (spoiler alert) we see that Luke was right. The good in Vader won out in the end. The Rebels' archenemy turned around and gave his own life for his son. Ahhh, what a moving moment a long time ago in a galaxy far, far away.

Not so with Satan. Fact: in this galaxy, in this day and time, Satan was and is a murderer from the get-go. He hates truth. There is absolutely no ounce of truth in him. Did you catch that? No good is in Satan—none, nada, zip, big goose egg. He *is* evil itself. Not even the mighty

Jedi warrior Luke Skywalker could draw out anything good from Satan.

- "(Satan) was a murderer from the beginning, and does not stand in the truth, because there is no truth in him. When he lies, he speaks out of his own character, for he is a liar and the father of lies." (John 8:44)
- "The great dragon was hurled down—that ancient serpent called the devil, or Satan, who leads the whole world astray." (Revelation 12:9 NIV '84)

Destroyed by Deception

Let's travel back in time to the Garden of Eden, just before Adam chose to sin. As the scene unfolds before us, we see our archenemy, Satan, beginning his attack by seeking to deceive Eve. Read that last statement again. Did you catch his battle plan?

When the Master Deceiver wanted to lead Adam and Eve into sin, he didn't stand over them with a sword, threatening to cut off their arms if they refused to do what he said. He didn't scream at them. He didn't torture them with bamboo shoved under their fingernails or by making them watch endless reruns of *I Love Lucy*. He simply started a seemingly innocent conversation focused on attacking Eve's mind. His goal: to change the way she thought about things.[7]

Now that's a critical point, here. He attacked Eve's *mind*. Satan knows that if he can impress your thinking, he can impact your living. Why? Because "as he thinks in his heart, so is he" (Proverbs 23:7 NKJV). What you think will eventually become what you do. When your thoughts are focused on King Me, your choices and actions will be for King Me. That's why we are commanded to take captive all our thoughts,[8] and think only on godly things.[9]

Satan's target is your mind. His weapon is lies. His purpose—to get you to live for King Me instead of God. Simply put, he wants to draw you away from the Almighty God of the Universe. He hates God, and he is going to try to use you to get to Him.

The steps Satan used on Eve in that garden are the same ones he uses on us today.

1. *He got Eve to question God's Word.*
   He began with a seemingly innocent question. He coyly asked her, "Did God really say what you think He said? What if you heard wrong? What if you're misinterpreting what He meant?" It was a simple question meant to cast doubt.

Potayto, Potahto

Notice Eve's response to what Satan said. "The woman said to the serpent, 'We may eat fruit from the trees in the garden ...'" (Genesis 3:2). Seems like an innocent enough response, right? However, look carefully at what she said to Satan. Can you see evidence that the seed of doubt has already begun to grow in Eve's mind?

- Step 1 of Eve's response: she took away from God's Word.

You see, God actually said, "You are free to eat from any tree in the garden ..." (Genesis 2:16). Can you see the subtle difference between what Eve said and what God said? It's there if you look for it. She left out one very important word. Did you find it yet? She neglected to tell Satan that she was "free" to eat from any tree in the garden.

"Seriously, now," you may ask, "are you really going to fuss over the omission of one small word?" Yup, I am. Jesus says in Matthew 5:18, "I tell you the truth, until heaven and earth disappear, not the smallest letter, not the least stroke of a pen, will by any means disappear from the Law until everything is accomplished." Luke recorded it this way, "It is easier for heaven and earth to disappear than for the least stroke of a pen to drop out of the Law" (Luke 16:17).

In other words, not only are the words of the Bible important to God; even the dotting of the "i's" and the crossing of the "t's" were inspired by God.[10] God views his Word very seriously, and so should we.

By removing the word "free," Eve made God into something He is not. She made God appear to be stingy, selfish, and uncaring. We must be very careful not to take away from God's Word. When we start down that path it becomes much easier to disobey God's will.

Give it Some Thought
- Read Psalm 119:11, 105; Proverbs 30:5; Hebrews 4:12; and 2 Timothy 3:16-17. Why did Satan want Eve to question the validity of God's Word?

- What's the danger of "rephrasing" Scripture?

Week 9, Day 4

Say It Ain't True

Hey, guys—yes I'm talking to you, Super Man of God—your archenemy wants to deceive your mind and draw you away from your Heavenly Father. He wants to get you to question God's Word. "Did God really say that?" When he can get you to doubt the truth of God's Word, he then bumps up his strategy to DefCon 2.

2. *He boldly denies God's Word.*
   "You will not surely die," he whispered in Eve's ear. You can almost hear the Devil's voice dripping with sarcasm. Can't you just see him snort at Eve's answer, roll his eyes as he says, "C'mon, do you really think you're going to 'die'? You're not going to die. Truth is, God's lying to you. He's not a very good God if He isn't telling you the whole truth."

Keep in mind that Adam and Eve had not seen death up to this point. They had no concept of it. But God had spoken, and all they needed to do was believe and obey. Hmm, something you and I should take to heart. Our responsibility isn't to understand the what, why, where, when or how of God's will, just believe and obey!

When you begin to question God's Word, it's not long before you begin to deny God's Word. When you begin to doubt the truth of what God says, it becomes easy for you to decide to do something other than what God says. Doubting God's truth will always lead to rejecting God's truth.

Once again, Eve's response is very revealing.

- Step 2 of Eve's response: She added to God's Word.

"God did say, 'You must not eat fruit from the tree that is in the middle of the garden, and you must not touch it, or you will die" (Genesis 3:3). Satan just called the Most Holy God, the Creator of the Universe, a big fat liar to her face. Did she tell Satan he was full of it and to get lost? Did she defend her creator and benefactor? Nope. The seed of doubt had already taken root. Her thoughts were pulling her farther away from the Truth. And so, she saw nothing wrong with adding her own spin to God's Word.

Consider what God had said. "You must not eat from the tree of the knowledge of good and evil, for when you eat of it you will surely die" (Genesis 2:17). Can you see what Eve added? She told Satan that God had said, "You must not *touch* it." Now where did that come from? Certainly not from God.

So, why was she wrong in adding to what God had said? After all, isn't it a good thing to not even touch the forbidden fruit? Hey dude, just steer clear of it completely and all is golden!

When Eve added to what God had said, she did two very serious things. First, she made God out to be less kind and giving. She stopped focusing on all that God had lovingly provided for them— hey, they had an entire garden at their disposal with more food than they could ever eat in a lifetime!

Instead, she zeroed in on the one thing she couldn't have. She set her thoughts solely on what God was withholding from her. The doubts in her mind began to solidify into thoughts of what she believed she deserved and what God was denying. God was infringing upon her rights. There really was no good reason why she couldn't eat of that fruit, other than the fact that God was just plain stingy and selfish.

The second thing she did when she added to God's Word was to make God's command a load too heavy for her to bear. Adding that additional restriction was just too much. I can almost hear her thinking: *"How could God possibly expect me to walk through the garden and not think about this particular tree? Doesn't He realize how hard it is for me to not just reach out and grab it?"*

God's commands are never a burden.[11] When Eve added to God's Word, she changed God's truth. It became something God never intended it to be—all about her. The Bible commands us to never add or subtract from Scripture.[12] God takes His Word seriously, and so should we.

Give it Some Thought
- All Adam and Eve had to do was believe and obey. Why is that so hard for us?

- How does questioning the validity and truth of God's Word lead to denying God's Word?

- Why do you think Eve added to God's Word?

- In what ways do we sometimes add to God's Word?

Week 9, Day 5

Back in the 1960s there was a popular TV show called *The Twilight Zone*. An episode entitled "The Howling Man"[13] tells the story of an American who goes on a walking trip through central Europe. Suddenly he is caught in a raging storm. Staggering through the blinding rain, he comes upon an impressive medieval castle—a home to a reclusive brotherhood of monks. They reluctantly take him in to provide shelter.

Later that night, the curious American decides to explore. Deep in the bowels of the castle, he finds a cell with a man locked inside. An ancient wooden staff lies across the door, holding it shut. The prisoner inside claims he is being held captive by the head monk, an insane man named Brother Jerome, and he pleads with the American to be merciful and release him.

The prisoner has a kindly face and a gentle voice. So the American, convinced the prisoner is being unjustly held against his will, confronts the head monk. Brother Jerome tells the American that the prisoner is none other than Satan himself, the father of lies. The wooden bar across the prison door is the Staff of Truth, the one and only barrier he cannot pass.

The American, now convinced the prisoner is right and Jerome is indeed mad, rushes to the prison door and removes the wooden Staff of Truth, thereby releasing the prisoner—who immediately transforms into a hideous, horned demon and vanishes in a puff of smoke.

The stunned American is horrified at the realization of what he has done and confesses his deed to Jerome. "I'm sorry for you, my son," Jerome responds. "All your life you will remember this night and whom you have turned loose upon the world."

"I didn't believe you," the American replies. "I saw him, but I didn't recognize him!"

"That," Jerome observes, "is man's weakness … and Satan's strength."

It's All A Lie – It's True!
The archenemy of your soul doesn't want you to live in victory over your sin. He doesn't want you living a godly life—what's the fun in that? So, he disguises himself and wages an all-out war against you. He attacks your mind with his lies to keep you from growing in your walk with God. Once he has you questioning the truth of God's Word, you begin to listen to his denial of God's Word. Then he moves in for the final blow.

3. *He inserts his own lies in place of God's Word, convincing you the lie is truth.*
   "God knows that if you eat the fruit of this tree, you will know the truth. You will see just what kind of God He really is. You will finally see how He's been using you. He doesn't care about you. In fact, He knows that if you eat that fruit, you will be like He is, and that threatens Him!"

Read Genesis 3:4-5. Can you identify the lie? Adam and Eve were already created after the image of God,[14] but Satan got them to question and then doubt that truth. Once they did that, it was easy for them to accept his lie substituted as being truth.

Sound familiar? Isn't that exactly how Satan works today? His M.O. (modus operandi) hasn't changed. Satan's lie, "You will be like God," still motivates and controls mankind today. Even as Super Men of God we are often sucked into that same mindset. Every time I put King Me on the throne of my heart, I am buying into the enemy's lie that I can control my life and I can determine my own destiny. I want, I need … I deserve!
- Moses said, "There is no one like the Lord our God." (Exodus 8:10)
- God said, "There is no one like me in all the earth." (Exodus 9:14)
- Samuel said, "How great you are, O Sovereign Lord! There is no one like you, and there is no God but you." (2 Samuel 7:22)
- David said, "There is no one like you, O Lord, and there is no God but you." (1 Chronicles 17:20)
- Again God said, "I am God, and there is no other; I am God and there is none like me." (Isaiah 46:9)

That is the truth that permeates Scripture. No one can be like God. Satan is a liar. And yet so many men, Christian men, Super Men of God, are believing the lie, trying to live in their own power and wisdom—turning to God only when their own efforts have failed them.

When we try to figure out life without looking to God's Word, when we attempt to make choices without seeking the guidance of our Heavenly Father, we become vulnerable to input from ungodly influences. Those influences will never lead us down the right path. They will try to sway us away from God.

When we begin to doubt God's Word and deny God's truth, when we allow Satan's deceitful lies to take the place of God's absolute truth, we will no longer see the necessity for God's Word. The result: we will begin to live a life apart from God's will.

By using the strategy he did, Satan convinced Eve to think about what that tree could do for her, instead of what God had already done. He influenced her thinking with his lies so that she doubted and questioned God's Word. That's when she was open to rejecting God's truth. The final blow came when she accepted Satan's lies as the truth and reached out, not only taking the fruit, but eating it as well.

Give it Some Thought
- Share with the guys at least one takeaway you received this week, and what you plan to do about it.

"But you are a chosen people, a royal priesthood, a holy nation, a people belonging to God, that you may declare the praises of him who called you out of darkness into his wonderful light."
1 Peter 2:9

Week 10
Who is Clark Kent, Anyway?

Week 10, Day 1

Some time had passed since Danny, Niah, Misha and Az were taken into captivity. They had finally settled into their new surroundings and adjusted to a new way of life, all the while maintaining their growing relationship with God. The result? God had richly blessed them.

The King took quite a fancy to Danny. Ol' King Nebby (which is what Danny liked to call him—when the King wasn't around, of course) gave Danny the name of Belteshazzar.[1] Not a very endearing name, but there you have it. Of course, Danny's God-given ability to interpret a rather annoying and elusive dream the King had[2] certainly helped propel the young man into stardom. You see, Danny was now ruler over the entire kingdom, a position of power just under the King himself. All the King's court reported to him: impressive, to say the least.

Niah, Misha and Az (now going by the names of Shad, Shack and Neggy[3]) had also been promoted. They were now high-ranking administrators over the kingdom.[4] Yup, they might be in a foreign land, surrounded by foreign people who didn't love God, let alone *know* Him, but those guys were doing pretty well. God had certainly blessed them, big time!

Bigger Than Life – Better to Die
As is the way with most stories in the Bible, the wicked King chose that very time to show his true colors. One day, Shad, Shack and

Neggy watched in total disbelief as the King's construction crew created a 90-foot high golden statue of himself. Did the King choose to put it in his garden so he could sit next to it and adore himself whenever the fancy hit him? Nope. Did he decide to put it in his bedroom so that as he fell to sleep at night he could remind himself of what a dynamic dictator he was? Unh-unh. He put it out where everyone could see it. He wasn't going to waste such handsomeness and awesomeness on just himself—no way. He was going to share himself for all to see and appreciate.

In a further stroke of genius (at least in his own mind), the King called all his government officials—including Shad, Shack and Neggy—to a very special dedication service. As the trio gathered in the courtyard, along with all of the other officials, Harvey the Herald stood next to the giant statue and cleared his throat. Oh, this was going to be interesting for sure.

"Hear ye, Hear ye! All satraps, prefects, governors, advisers, treasurers, judges, magistrates and all other provincial officials. His most royal, most grand and glorious King is giving you this command. From this time forward, every time you hear the sound of the horn, flute, zither, lyre, harp and pipes playing the imperial theme song, you all are hereby commanded to immediately stop what you are doing, fall down on to your face, and worship the golden image of your King."

In the brief moment of silence that followed, everyone heard Neggy snort and say, "Yah, like that's gonna happen." Without skipping a beat, Harvey continued. "Whoever does *not* fall down and worship will immediately be thrown into a blazing furnace." As Harvey rolled up his scroll, he glared at Neggy and then pushed his way through the murmuring crowd. The three friends stood in silent shock. Well, that was a fine how-do-you-do. How were they going to handle this one?

Unfortunately, Danny was away on a business trip, so they couldn't talk to him about it. What would Danny do? Better yet, what would God want them to do? There really was no question. Deep in their hearts they knew what had to be done.

Just as the crowd was leaving to head back to work, the musicians began playing the imperial theme song (no, not the one from Star

Wars—wrong storyline). Everyone stopped, dropped and worshipped the golden image. Everyone, that is, except Shad, Shack and Neggy.

The ground was a blanket of people on their knees, bent forward, worshipping the golden statue. The three rebels stood out like a blister on a camel's nose in the mid-afternoon sun. King Nebby was furious —demanding that those three be brought before him immediately.

> # Hebrews 7:25
> *"Consequently, he is able to save to the uttermost those who draw near to God through him, since he always lives to make intercession for them."*

"I know that you boys have refused to serve my gods, and I've been lenient up till now. But are you seriously refusing to worship my image of gold?" He paused, looking each one in the eyes, daring them to disobey his next directive. "I'll give you one more chance to redeem yourselves. The next time you hear the imperial theme song played, I order you to fall down and worship my image. If you do, I'll forgive you. But if you don't …!"

Shad bowed his head toward the King as a sign of respect, then said, "O great and wonderful King. I know we stand accused before you of this crime, but we have no need to defend ourselves in this matter. The fact is, we will not bow down before your image—not today, not tomorrow, not ever. If you choose to throw us into the blazing furnace, so be it. We know that the one true God we serve is more than able to save us from it, and you."

The King's face turned beet red as anger filled his spirit. Just as he was about to pass his verdict, Neggy stepped forward. "But even if our God chooses not to save us, we want you to know, O King, that we will never serve your gods or worship your image of gold, because they are not God!"[5]

As far as Ol' King Nebby was concerned, it was a done deal. They had definitely crossed the line. Ordering their execution wasn't easy for him, as he had grown to like those boys. But rebellion is rebellion, and it had to be nipped in the bud. He ordered the furnace cranked up to full—higher than it had ever gone.

Everyone gathered around expectantly, anxious to see justice done to those three Hebrew rebels. Four of the royal guard stepped forward at the King's command, grabbed Shad, Shack and Neggy, and pushed them toward the raging furnace. Binding their hands behind their back, the guards led the boys up the steps to the top of the blazing inferno.

As Shad, Shack and Neggy climbed the stairs, they could feel the intense heat. Reaching the top, they could see the flames dancing inside the furnace and they could hear the deafening roar. Glancing at each other, drawing strength from their collective resolve to serve God to the very end, they fell into the furnace.

Hitting the bottom with a thud, Shack was surprised to open his eyes and see that he was still alive. Looking around he saw Shad and Neggy standing, too, and walking toward him. Then it hit him—they weren't dead! In fact, they weren't burning. Their clothes weren't even on fire! The three of them embraced, laughing at the miracle God was giving them. That's when Shack noticed a fourth person in the furnace with them. Was it one of the royal guards? Squinting, leaning forward in an attempt to get a closer look, Shack shouted out above the roar of the flames, "Guys—hey, guys, we're not alone!"

Turning to look where Shack was pointing, they saw the very God they loved and served coming toward them. When he drew them into his arms, they wept and rejoiced at what God was doing in their lives. They had stood up for Him, and now He was standing up with them.

Give it Some Thought
- In what ways have you found it difficult to live as Teknon Theos, as an alien in this wicked world?

- What spiritual challenges do you face daily?

- Why do you qualify them as "challenges"—what makes them challenging?

- When the world puts pressure on us to "worship" what they do, and the way they do it, why do Christians tend to buckle under that pressure and give in?

- What are some ways we can fight that urge to give in?

- Why were Shad, Shack and Neggy able to stand true to their convictions, even as they were being tossed into the fiery furnace?

- What do you need to do to have that same resolve?

Week 10, Day 2

The low, menacing rumble was growing in volume and intensity. Danny closed his eyes tightly. A cold chill ran up his spine for the umpteenth time that night. Oh, he groaned inwardly, was this nightmare ever going to end? Danny knew God was with him. He knew that whatever happened tonight, God would be glorified. That gave Danny an inner peace he could never have imagined possible in a situation like this.

As he knelt in the mud mixed with urine and feces, Danny could sense a powerful presence creeping up behind him, slowly, methodically inching its way closer and closer. Again, the rumble. Suddenly he felt the hot breath of the beast on the back of his neck as it pressed its cold nose against his flesh. Sniffing, exhaling, then sniffing again. Then that nerve-wracking rumble. Danny prayed, and prayed hard. It was all he could do to keep his fear at bay. Every fiber in him wanted to scream and run. He had nowhere he could go but to God.

The beast circled him deliberately, frustrated that his prey was right in front of him, yet completely untouchable. Again the rumble, deep and throaty. A second beast was there (possibly even a third—Danny couldn't tell for sure), just a few feet away, sitting in the darkness, watching him. Danny could hear it breathing. He swore he could even hear its heart beat. The sound of it licking its paw was maddening.

Shifting his weight to keep his legs from falling asleep under him, again, Danny kicked a pile of bones left from the beast's previous meal. The stench of rotting flesh filled the den, making Danny want to retch. But he had already emptied the contents of his stomach hours ago. The rumble from deep within the beast's chest echoed in the dank den. Danny continued to pray.

He half chuckled to himself as the massive, hungry lion nudged his shoulder and then sniffed his neck again. Prayer. That's what landed him here to begin with. But he'd have it no other way.

48 Hours Earlier

King Nebby was long gone. In his place was King Darius, a Persian who didn't care about rugs, or about anything his predecessor had done. The moment Darius had taken office he made changes—significant changes. Danny was no longer second-in-command. Darius had divided the land into 120 different provinces, and placed governors over each of them. Ruling over the governors were three administrators—Darius' right-hand men. Danny was one of those three.

In the weeks and months after the Persian takeover, God had once again blessed Danny to the point where Darius was seriously considering giving him his old job back as second-in-command over the entire kingdom. When news got out about the pending promotion, the other two administrators, along with the 120 governors, weren't very pleased with the thought of having to answer to a Hebrew.

They got together and conspired to find some legal action they could take against Danny. Demotion wasn't enough, though. Prison was too good for him. No, he needed to die. Try as they might, they couldn't find anything worthy of a death sentence. His books were in order, his record-keeping was flawless. All his business dealings were honest and aboveboard. This guy was squeaky clean. He was neither corrupt nor negligent in anything he did.[6] This wasn't going to be easy.

In one of their secret meetings, someone suggested that if they were going to find something with which to frame Danny, it would need to have something to do with the laws of his God. They watched Danny closely over the next few days. Like a lion crouched in the grass near a herd of grazing deer, they watched, waiting for the right moment to pounce. Then they found it.

Danny had an annoying habit of kneeling at his window three times a day to pray to his God. Every day, at the same time each day, he prayed. That was it! That was their opening. Quickly they put together their plan, then ran to the King.

"Oh, King Darius," their voices dripped with flattery. "We've been talking about how fantastic a ruler you are. We've never had a King as wonderful as you. In fact, you've become a god to us! We think you should issue an edict, a decree that requires everyone in your kingdom to pray to you. And if anyone prays to any god or man besides you, they should immediately be thrown into the lion's den!"[7]

Darius didn't notice the looks being passed between his governors, or he would have known they were up to something. Instead, full of pride, he just closed his eyes, sat back on his throne and dreamt of what it would be like to have his entire kingdom worship him. And why not? He *was* a god to them, after all.

When Danny learned that the decree had been issued, he went home to his upstairs room, opened the window and prayed. Three times that day he prayed, just like he always did.[8] Three times he knelt before his Creator, asking the one true God for direction and help.

Just after supper there was a rush of footsteps outside and a pounding on his door. As he opened the door, palace guards pushed their way in, grabbed Danny and dragged him before the King.

"Oh Danny boy, my dear, dear boy, what have you done?" Darius moaned. Since the moment he heard that Danny had been praying to his God, and that the guards were sent to capture him, the King was heartbroken. He tried to find some way, some loophole in the law, anything that could save Danny from certain death. But he found nothing. "You have given me no choice, Danny, but to order your death. May your God whom you serve so faithfully figure out a way to rescue you, because I cannot."[9]

Morning Has Broken
So here was Danny, circled by extremely frustrated and hungry lions who wanted nothing more than to enjoy a late night Danny-burger, on his knees praying to God for help.

Again that rumble, only this time it was different. It wasn't coming from the lions. Unsure at first of what he was hearing, Danny looked up to see a crack of light peeking through. The stone that covered the den was being removed.

Shielding his eyes from the bright light that was now pouring into the den, Danny heard Darius shouting desperately. "Danny? Danny? Was your God able to do what I could not? Was he able to save you from the lions?" Danny could hear the concern and anguish in the King's voice. Smiling to himself he shouted back, "O King, live forever! My God sent his angel last night, and he shut the mouths of the lions. They have not hurt me because I was innocent in God's sight. I have not done anything wrong, O King!"[10]

Give it Some Thought

- Once he knew of the king's edict, why did Daniel still choose to go to his window to pray? Why didn't he change tactics and just go to his closet to pray?

- When faced with a similar situation, what might you do and why?

- What is prayer?

- What is the purpose of prayer?

- When you pray, what do you typically talk to God about? Why?

Week 10, Day 3

We've taken a brief glimpse into the lives of four men named Daniel, Shadrach, Meshach and Abednego. Four men who were Super Men of God. Four men who faced the enemy and, against all odds, came out the victors.

- What made those four guys "Super Men"? Why were they able to stand firm in the face of certain defeat?

- What commonality do you share with these guys?

Who Is That Guy?

When he's not being confused with a bird or a plane, Clark Kent works as a journalist with some very clumsy tendencies, to throw off others from knowing his true identity as Superman.

Matthew 5:14-16

"You are the light of the world. A city set on a hill cannot be hidden. Nor do people light a lamp and put it under a basket, but on a stand, and it gives light to all in the house. In the same way, let your light shine before others, so that they may see your good works and give glory to your Father who is in heaven."

The disguise of Clark Kent is actually quite thorough, when you think about it. Clark is registered as a natural-born citizen. He votes. He has jealousies and shortcomings. He has opinions that he's willing to share. He has appropriately nerdy hobbies (he does scrapbooking, for goodness' sake). He collects his favorite classic television commercials on DVD.

Clark doesn't just wear glasses; he behaves completely differently than Superman. He changes his voice, combs his hair differently, wears loose-fitting clothing to hide his physique. He slouches, uses different mannerisms, and is in situations where nobody expects to see Superman—at a desk job, acting weak and normal, buying cauliflower at the grocery store and renting old movies.

Consider, for a moment, the names Tony Stark and Bruce Wayne. Depending on how nerdy you are, those names may or may not mean anything to you. For the less-educated in superhero lore, Tony Stark is Iron Man, and Bruce Wayne is Batman. Both Tony and Bruce live normal, everyday lives as themselves. Tony and Bruce are the real deal. However, when needed, Tony becomes Iron Man and Bruce becomes Batman. Here's my point: to become their alter egos, unlike Superman they must put on the costume and assume that role.

Superman, on the other hand, must remove his costume (the persona of Clark Kent) to be the Superman that he already is. Anytime the man of steel is needed, as he rushes to the emergency, he rips open his shirt and tie to reveal what lies underneath his costume. The guy in the blue outfit with the big red **S** emblazoned on his chest is the real Superman (Kal-El). Superman can't do the stuff that Clark can do. Why? Because he's Superman; because Superman would never do those things. So Kal-El puts on the costume of Clark Kent to fit in with the world around him and be accepted as one of them.

Throughout this study we have seen that as a born-again believer, YOU already are a Super Man of God. Your real identity is Teknon Theos (son of God). You don't need to put on a costume to become a Super Man of God because that's who you already are. But let's face it, guys; we do wear a costume, don't we? The costume isn't one of spiritual superhero-dom. The costume isn't one of being a godly Christian guy. No, it's the costume of our humanness. It's the costume that enables us to fit in with the world around us so we don't draw unwanted attention.

- Superman wore glasses, over-sized clothing, and changed his voice and hairstyle, all so he could fit in. What are some of the things we tend to "put on" to fit in?

- Read Galatians 1:10. Why do we do that—why do we put on a costume to fit in with the rest of the world?

- 2 Corinthians 6:17 commands us to "come out from (the world) and be separate." Exodus 23:2 says, "Do not follow the crowd in doing wrong." Why?

Listen to the instruction Peter gives: "(Don't) live the rest of your life for evil human desires, but rather for the will of God. For you have spent enough time in the past doing what pagans choose to do … They think it strange that you do not plunge with them into the same flood … and they heap abuse on you. But they will have to give account to him who is ready to judge the living and the dead" (1 Peter 4:2-5).

We have a choice. We can choose to "live in order to please God,"[11] or put on the costume and "conform to the evil desires (we) had when (we) lived in ignorance."[12] We can choose to "live as children of light"[13] and be "the light of the world,"[14] or put on the costume, effectively putting our light under a basket.[15]

What choice are you making? Please note I did not ask, "What choice *will* you make?" You have already chosen. Your task, should you choose to accept, is to remove the costume once and for all, and live as the Super Man of God your creator intends you to be.[16]

"But I don't know how to 'be' a Super Man of God!" you say. Let me help you get started. Read the following verses, and in your own words write out what you need to do to be God's man of steel.
• Ephesians 5:1

• 1 Thessalonians 4:1, 3-5

• Galatians 5:1

• Romans 13:12-14

• Galatians 5:16

- 2 Timothy 2:21

Week 10, Day 4

Throughout this study, we've talked about being a superhero. We've looked at Superman and have seen four primary points:

1. Superman is an alien from another planet—this world is not his home. Fortunately, he has a Fortress of Solitude that enables him to check in with his father and talk with him about how to live as an alien among a people who don't understand him.

2. Superman has amazing powers, all because of his proximity to Earth's yellow sun. Without the sun, he has no ability to fight off the enemies who want to take him down.

3. Superman is vulnerable to Kryptonite—chunks of his past. Kryptonite is the only thing that can weaken him. As long as he stays away from his Kryptonite, all is golden.

4. Superman is always Superman. To hide his real identity and fit in with the world around him, he dons the costume of mild-mannered Clark Kent, reporter for the Daily Planet.

From those four aspects of Superman, we have learned four truths about us as Super Men of God:

1. As a child of God, you are an alien. This world is not your home. Your citizenship is in heaven.[17] You have been given a "fortress of solitude" (prayer and God's word) that enables you to spend time with your Heavenly Father and talk with him about how to live as an alien amongst a people who don't understand you.

2. As a Super Man of God, you have amazing powers[18]—you can say "No!" to the enemy, standing firm in your faith, resisting him and watch him flee from you.[19] The only way you can maintain that power is to stay close to the Son of God, daily maintaining a growing relationship with Christ.

3. You have a "Kryptonite" that can spiritually weaken you, making you vulnerable to the attacks of the enemy. It's your past—past temptations, past sins, a past life that calls out to you, crying for attention. You must stay away from it at all costs.[20]

4. As a born-again believer, you are always Teknon Theos (a child of God). The only way you can fit in with the world around you is to put on a "costume" and pretend to be like them.[21]

We have also learned that the archenemy of your soul is trying to destroy you. We are at war, my friend. We are daily engaged in spiritual warfare, and at times it can be exhausting, right? How is the battle going for you?

- Review: Remember your list of FROGS (your Kryptonite)? Why do those particular things cause you such grief?

Battle-Ready

It's important we never forget that our battle isn't against other men. Our battle is against the evil of hell itself.[22] Satan has one up on you: he has centuries of experience under his belt. He started this whole battle with Eve. Just as he did with her, so he is trying to lead your thoughts away from being fully focused on Christ.[23]

At times this war can feel overwhelming, I know. That's when I like to read this promise from God:

"When you go out to war against your enemies, and see horses and chariots and an army larger than your own, you shall not be afraid of them, for the Lord your

> God is with you, who brought you up out of the land
> of Egypt." (Deuteronomy 20:1)

Consider this: God has already delivered you out of the very pit of hell itself. He has adopted you as His child![24] He has given you an amazing inheritance that no one can take away from you.[25] Do you really think He is going to let you flounder and be massacred by the enemy?[26]

This war can feel defeating at times. It's then that you need to remember:

> "Neither death, nor life, nor angels nor rulers, nor
> things present nor things to come, nor powers, nor
> height nor depth, nor anything else in all creation
> (including your archenemies), will be able to separate
> us from the love of God in Christ Jesus our
> Lord." (Romans 8:38-39, addition mine)

That's powerful! As Teknon Theos, as a Super Man of God, you can fight and win! You can do it through Christ because He will give you all the strength you need.[27]

Give it Some Thought
- Name some ways that putting on your "costume" prevents you from being a Super Man of God."

- What are some ways this week you can show to the world around you that you are Teknon Theos?

Based on your answer to the above question, let's make a covenant together as a group of men that we will hold each other accountable to this.

Week 10, Day 5

Big G was intimidating. No, not intimidating—dominating. He was, without question, the bully of the century, and everyone in high school knew it. He had developed early in life and stood taller than the tallest basketball player on their team, and weighed more than the heaviest wrestler they had. He was big, solid, and had a cruel streak that was meaner than a wolverine and Tasmanian devil combined.

The day Big G met his match was a hot, hot Saturday afternoon in August. It hadn't rained in over a month. The ball field was a dust bowl. Every step kicked up a cloud of dirt that caked the inside of your nostrils and dried the back of your throat. Big G and his band of followers had just stormed out on to the field, disrupting the game.

"C'mon, G!" the kids began to shout. "Off the field! We're trying to play a game here!"

"Yeah?" Big G taunted them, "Who's gonna make me?" No one moved. "That's what I thought. You're nuttin' but a bunch of cowards. Make ya' a deal. Send one person over here to fight me. If he wins, we leave. But if I win, you bunch-o-losers have to leave and never come back!"

Still no one moved. Not even the wind. Sweat was flowing and hearts were pounding. It appeared, once again, that Big G was gonna win. Suddenly a scrawny little freshman pushed his way through the crowd and started walking across the field.

A murmur began to grow in the crowd. "Who is that little kid, and what on earth does he think he's doing? Doesn't he know that's Big G? Big G's gonna pulverize him. Somebody should stop him!" But nobody did. They all stood in disbelief as the skinny, short, snot-nosed nobody marched right up to the pitcher's mound.

"You heard us, Big G. Get off the field. We're not going to let you ruin our game. Now move, or else!"

Big G just stared at the kid in disbelief. Finally, he began to laugh. It wasn't a funny, ha-ha kind of laugh. It was a menacing, maniacal, rattle-your-bones-in-fear kind of laugh. Everyone knew what that laugh meant. That scraggly little kid standing all alone on the pitcher's mound was dead meat.

Suddenly the freshman reached down, picked up a rock and pitched it right at Big G. It wasn't a lob, it wasn't a toss; it was a pitch—better, faster and stronger than Nolan Ryan, Randy Johnson and Roger Clemens combined. You could hear it sing as it zipped through the air, and before Big G could react the stone landed smack dab in the middle of his forehead, knocking him flat on the ground.

The kids came pouring out of the dugout, rushing to the pitcher's mound and their unlikely hero. "Who is this kid?" everyone asked, "and how on earth did he do that?"

"My name is David," came the reply. "And I just did what my father taught me to do. I trusted in the fact that as long as I did what he taught me, I would be perfectly fine!"

The reason David could defeat Goliath[28] is simply because David, a scrawny little shepherd boy, knew that he was Teknon Theos. As a Super Man of God, as a man who maintained a close relationship with the Son, as a man who trusted in all that his Heavenly Father taught him to do, he was able to step onto the battlefield with a stone and a sling and, in the name of God, defeat the big bully.

Guys, be the men God has called you to be. "Today you are drawing near for battle against your enemies: let not your heart faint. Do not fear or panic or be in dread of them, for the Lord your God is he who goes with you to fight for you against your enemies, to give you the victory" (Deuteronomy 20:3-4).

All through Scripture we see that God has given victory where defeat and destruction seemed inevitable. God hasn't changed. God will never change.[29] That means that He stands ready, right here and now, to give you victory over the giant in your life.[30] So take off that costume you're wearing and let the world see you for who you really are!

Give it Some Thought

- Read 2 Samuel 22:1-4. What did David do when he defeated his enemies?

- How can you apply that principle to your life?

- Share with the guys at least one takeaway you received from this week, and what you plan to do about it.

"Do not be conformed to this world, but be transformed
by the renewal of your mind, that by testing you may discern
what is the will of God, what is good and acceptable and perfect."
Romans 12:2

Week 11
The Keys to Being a Super Man of God

In any Superman movie, there is the inevitable scene that shows Clark Kent either entering a phone booth as the mild-mannered reporter and stepping out as Superman, or simply removing his glasses and ripping open his shirt to reveal the red **S** emblazoned on his chest.

Either way, we know we're about to see our superhero in action.

Do I Have to Rip Open My Shirt?
Throughout this study, you have learned that as a child of God you already are a Super Man. You have all the power you need to *be* a godly man of purity and integrity. You are fully equipped to fight the battle and stand victoriously over the fallen enemy.

The biggest problem we run into is simply this: doubt. Because of your constant exposure to temptation, because of your previous falls and failures, because of your humanness, you struggle to believe that you can be victorious. You battle with skepticism, unsure if God is really referring to *you* when He says that we are more than conquerors.[1] You lack the confidence to step out, stand firm, and resist the Devil.[2]

This week we are going to focus on an amazing truth found in Scripture. This truth will help you discover that your fears and frustrations are unfounded and unnecessary. In fact, as you study this truth, you will uncover the secret to being a Super Man of God—and no, you don't have to rip open your shirt!

"Do not be conformed to this world, but be transformed by the renewal of your mind, that by testing you may discern what is the will of God, what is good and acceptable and perfect." Romans 12:2

On the next page, you will see a diagram. As you work your way through this week's study, think long and hard about what you've been learning over the last ten weeks. Using the diagram and the notes that follow, determine your next steps—what are you going to do from this point forward? How are you going to apply what you've learned? How are you going to show to the world around you that you are Teknon Theos—a Super Man of God?

Note: each day's study corresponds to the numbers on the diagram.

Being A Super Man of God

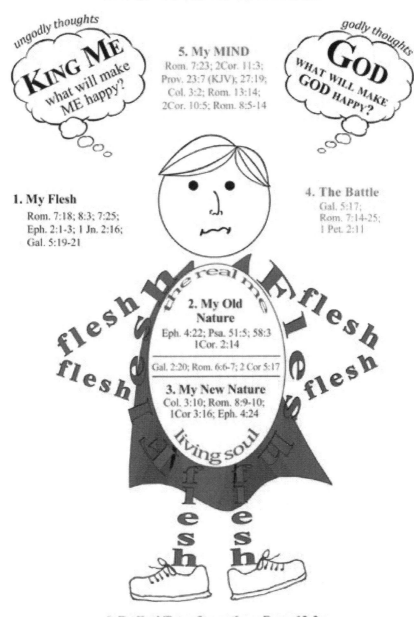

6. Radical Transformation - Rom. 12:2

Week 11, Day 1

1. My Flesh

When you look in the mirror, what do you see? Be honest, now. What do you see? Did you ever stop to think that what you are seeing is not really you? Okay, if you want to get technical, when you look at a mirror you're seeing a reflection—but that's not what I'm talking about. The image reflected in the mirror is not you. It's just your body. It's just a vehicle to travel through life in. It's not the real you.

The real you lives *inside* your body. The Apostle Paul calls it your "inner being" (or inner man).[3] It's the part of you that God cares about deeply—so deeply that He paid the ultimate price to save the real you from an eternity in Hell (see John 3:16; Romans 5:8; and 2 Corinthians 5:21).

When God looks at you, my friend, He's not looking at your body— He's looking at your soul. Your Heavenly Father "sees not as man sees: man looks on the outward appearance, but the Lord looks on the heart" (1 Samuel 16:7). Man looks at your body, your flesh, and tends to judge you by your looks as well as your successes and failures. But God sees what's inside. He sees the real you. Your inner being is what matters to Him, and He wants the real you to be totally focused on Him.[4] That's when the Holy Spirit strengthens you with His power to be the Super Man of God you are supposed to be.[5]

> ## Galatians 5:16
> *"But I say, walk by the Spirit, and you will not gratify the desires of the flesh."*

The problem is your sinful flesh. That's what is keeping you from living as the man of steel God created you to be. So let's talk for a few moments about your flesh.

Paul said, "I know that nothing good dwells in me, that is, *in my flesh.* For I have the desire to do what is right, but not the ability to carry it out" (Romans 7:18, emphasis mine). Can you relate? You want to do what is right. You want to live a life that glorifies God. You want to be a Super Man of God, yet your sinful flesh keeps getting in the way. You struggle to live out the godliness you feel inside.

- Read Galatians 5:19-21. From the list in this verse, what are the "works of the flesh" that you tend to struggle with?

- What do those things "do" for you? In other words, why do you do them?

- Now read Colossians 3:1-10. As a child of God, what are you supposed to do with the works of the flesh?

> ## Ephesians 2:3
> *"We all once lived in the passions of our flesh, carrying out the desires of the body and the mind, and were by nature children of wrath."*

Have you ever driven a car that's out of alignment? When you let go of the steering wheel, what happens? It pulls the vehicle to the right or to the left. It naturally wants to go where you don't want it to go. If you let go of the wheel, disaster is bound to happen. To keep it on a straight path, you must put both hands on the steering wheel and continuously fight the pull.

As a child of God (as Teknon Theos) you are in a constant battle with your flesh. That is because your flesh is weakened by sin.[6] Your flesh has a natural bent toward sin. The fact is, "While we (are) in the flesh, the sinful passions … (are) at work in the members of our body to bear fruit for death" (Romans 7:5). Your flesh is the vehicle you use to travel through life, and it's permanently out of alignment. When you "let go of the wheel" it will always pull you away from God.

Paul described it this way: "The desires of the flesh are against the Spirit, and the desires of the Spirit are against the flesh, for these are opposed to each other, to keep you from doing the things you want to do" (Galatians 5:17).

Give it Some Thought
• Why the conflict? Why is there such a struggle with my sinful flesh? (For help, read 1 John 2:16.)

• Read each verse below, then write a brief summary of how it applies to this study.

"For I know that nothing good dwells in me, that is, in my flesh. For I have the desire to do what is right, but not the ability to carry it out." (Romans 7:18)

"We all once lived in the passions of our flesh, carrying out the desires of the body and the mind, and were by nature children of wrath, like the rest of mankind." (Ephesians 2:3)

"For if you live according to the flesh you will die." (Romans 8:13a)

Week 11, Day 2

2. I Was Born Dead (I Had an Old Sinful Nature)

Brothers Ethan and Evan were known around town as being less-than-honest businessmen. Between their crooked business dealings and connections to the mafia, they were mean and cold-blooded. You definitely didn't want to do business with them, and if you did, you did so at great risk not just to your bottom line but to your personal well-being.

One day Evan had a massive heart attack and died. Ethan wanted to give his dear brother a funeral that would be remembered for ages to come. He spared no expense. Working with the funeral home, he made all the arrangements except one: he couldn't find a preacher who would do the memorial service.

Finally, he found a pastor of a small community church who was willing—if Ethan would donate $15,000 to put a new roof on the church. Ethan agreed on one condition. In the pastor's eulogy, he had to call Evan a "Saint." The preacher agreed.

Curiosity got the better of the town, and everyone showed up for the funeral service. As the music stopped and the preacher stood, the silence in the room was complete. Everyone wondered what he would say. Ethan looked at the preacher. The preacher looked at Ethan, cleared his throat and began.

"Today we are here to acknowledge the man we all knew as Evan. Evan was an evil man. He was a liar, a thief, a deceiver, a manipulator, and a hedonist. All he cared about was himself. He destroyed the fortunes, careers, and lives of countless people in this town. Evan did every self-centered, egotistical, rotten thing you can think of—and many others you can't even begin to imagine. But compared to his brother, Evan was indeed a saint!" (*source unknown*)

Although we might get a slight chuckle from that story, we also know there's an element of truth to it. I'm not saying that every human being is just as corrupt, just as wicked, just as despicable as everyone else; that would not be true.

However, every one of us was born with a wicked, old sinful nature. On the day you were conceived, you were a sinner. On the day you were born, you were a sinner. Truth be told, you were born dead. Without Christ you were alive physically, but dead spiritually. You would have been accurately described as the walking dead. Why? Because "the wages of sin is death" (Romans 6:23a).

David wrote, "Surely I was *sinful at birth*, sinful from the time my mother conceived me" (Psalm 51:5). And Paul says very matter-of-factly that before salvation we were all "dead in trespasses and sins."[8]

It's important here that you understand this: you weren't born "neutral." You didn't come into this world with the possibility of going one way or the other. You were born a sinner. You were born with an old, sinful nature. A person doesn't become a thief when he steals; he steals because he already is a thief. A person doesn't become a liar when he tells a lie; he tells a lie because he already is a liar. "Even *from birth* the wicked go astray; *from the womb* they are wayward and speak lies" (Psalm 58:3).

Remember, the flesh is just the shell—the vehicle that travels through life carrying the real you inside of it. Without Christ, the real you is dead, lifeless, without hope of being with God in Heaven for eternity. Look at these verses and consider the point that Paul is making:

"Those who live according to the flesh set their minds on the things of the flesh." (Romans 8:5)

"To set the mind on the flesh is death." (Romans 8:6)

"The mind that is set on the flesh is hostile to God, for it does not submit to God's law; indeed, it cannot." (Romans 8:7)

"If you live according to the flesh you will die." (Romans 8:13)

Your old, sinful nature had no desire for, or devotion to, God in any way, shape or form because it was dead in sin. It focused entirely on one thing: gratifying the sinful cravings of your flesh. Anything the flesh wanted, the old nature was willing to provide.

Paul is telling us that before salvation your thoughts were focused on fulfilling the sinful desires of the flesh. As we will discuss on day five of this week, what you think strongly influences what you do. With your mind set on fulfilling the sinful desires of the flesh, you lived a life characterized by sinful choices. Without Christ, your mind had nothing holy and godly to help direct its thinking.

However, when you placed your faith in Jesus Christ as your Savior, something very interesting happened. What happened, you ask? We'll take a closer look at it tomorrow!

Give it Some Thought
- Read each verse below, then write a brief summary of how it applies to this study.

  "And you were dead in the trespasses and sins in which you once walked, following the course of this world, following the prince of the power of the air, the spirit that is now at work in the sons of disobedience—among whom we all once lived in the passions of our flesh, carrying out the desires of the body and the mind, and were by nature children of wrath, like the rest of mankind." (Ephesians 2:1-3)

  "Put off your old self, which belongs to your former manner of life and is corrupt through deceitful desires." (Ephesians 4:22)

Week 11, Day 3

3. Upon Salvation, I Was Given a New Nature

The very moment you placed your faith in Jesus Christ as your Savior, something wonderful happened.

"I have been crucified with Christ. It is no longer I who live, but Christ who lives in me. And the life I now live in the flesh I live by faith in the Son of God, who loved me and gave himself for me." (Galatians 2:20)

• Take note of Paul's use of the words "*have been crucified*" in the verse above. How would you define the word "crucified?"

• When something is dead, what does that mean?

• Can that which is crucified/dead ever come back to life?

Paul very clearly says "I" have been crucified, and "I" no longer live. If crucified means dead, gone, never to come back, then who (or what) died? I ask simply because Paul is very much alive as he writes the words of Galatians 2:20. Yet he says he is dead; he no longer lives. What died? What is no longer around? What can never come back to life again?

To answer that, let's look at Romans 6:6-7. "We know that *our old self was crucified* with him in order that the body of sin might be brought to nothing, so that we would no longer be enslaved to sin. For one who has died has been set free from sin" (emphasis mine).

It's your old sinful nature that was crucified. That old nature was put to death when you put your faith in Christ. So, on the diagram, identify #2: "My Old Nature," and draw an "X" through the top half of "the real me"—cross out all of #2 to remind you that part of you no longer exists.

"Therefore, if anyone is in Christ, he is a *new creation*. The *old has passed away*; behold, the new has come."
(2 Corinthians 5:17, emphasis mine)

The words "passed away" means simply to perish, to come to an end, to cease to exist. Once again, a solid statement that the old, sinful nature is dead and gone. I find it very interesting that twice now Paul refers to the sinful nature as being "old." That word "old" doesn't refer to chronological age, but rather to that which you had from the beginning: the original thing. In other words, that which you were born with—your old sinful nature. The moment you were saved, that old nature died.

"But Steve, I still sin!" Yes, you do—and so do I. However, as a born-again believer, you are not sinning *because* you still have an old sinful nature. You are sinning because you still live in a sinful body.

> ## 2 Corinthians 5:17
> *"Therefore, if anyone is in Christ, he is a new creation. The old has passed away; behold, the new has come."*

After that old, sinful nature was crucified, what then? What happened after that? Paul answers: "if anyone is in Christ, he is a NEW CREATION." Another way of putting it: you have been Born Again! This is why Paul says we are to "Put on the *new self*, which is being renewed in knowledge after the image of its *creator*" (Colossians 3:10, emphasis mine).

God didn't take your old nature and refurbish it. He didn't give it a makeover. He didn't drag it into His shop and do a major overhaul on it. He completely annihilated it and *created* a brand-spankin' new one to take its place.

Then, He—the Almighty, Most Holy, Sovereign God of the Universe—moved in! Yup, He set up His throne room in your heart! Look again at Galatians 2:20. Yes, you were crucified with Christ. Yes, the old sinful nature no longer lives. But then what? Christ now lives IN you!

> "You, however, are not in the flesh but in the Spirit, if in fact *the Spirit of God dwells in you*. Anyone who does not have the Spirit of Christ does not belong to him. But if <u>Christ is in you</u>, although *the <u>body is dead</u> because of sin, the <u>Spirit is life</u> because of righteousness*." (Romans 8:9-10, emphasis mine)

> "Don't you know that you yourselves are God's temple and that God's Spirit lives in you?" 1 Corinthians 3:16

If you are a born-again believer, God has taken up residency inside of you. He dwells *in* you, my friend! But how on earth is that possible? How can a holy God who cannot even look at sin[11] permanently camp out in you—especially when you battle with sin every day of your life? The answer is: your new nature. In order for God to dwell within you, He had to remove the old sinful nature and put a new, holy nature in its place. If your new nature could sin, God couldn't live there.[12]

- Notice that your new nature was *created* by God (not refurbished). Why is that so important?

- Your new nature was created "after" (literally "according to") the likeness of God. In other words, it's a direct reflection or exact representation of God. What's so significant about that?

Finally, notice that your new nature was created in "true holiness"—literally, "perfect purity." In other words: your new nature is perfectly pure, incapable of sinning! Consider this: God is holy. We just saw that your new nature was created according to God's holiness. Therefore, your new nature is a HOLY nature!

Give it Some Thought
- When the Bible says God is Holy (e.g., 1 Samuel 2:2; Isaiah 6:3; 57:15; Revelation 4:8), what does that mean?

- God's holiness means more than just that God doesn't sin. It means He is totally incapable of sinning. God and sin are at polar opposites of each other. And your new nature was created after God's holy nature. Write out your thoughts—what does that truth mean for you?

Note: if you would like to learn more about this, please read my book *Extreme Mind Makeover: How to Transform Sinful Thoughts and Habits Into God-Pleasing Patterns of Life,* Overboard Ministries, 2011.

Week 11, Day 4

4. Let the Battle Begin!
Have you ever wondered why you do some of the sinful things you do? Ever ask yourself, *"What was I thinking?"* Hey, we've all been there, my friend. Even the apostle Paul battled with this issue.
- Read Romans 7:15-25. Write below the verses that resonate with you. In Paul's description, what can you relate to?

Did you notice that Paul speaks of two different "I's"? He says the things "I" want to do, "I" don't do—and the things "I" don't want to do, those are the things "I" go ahead and do. Is Paul battling with multiple personalities? Is he schizophrenic? Nope. He's simply describing the same struggle every Christian faces: the battle between the sinful flesh and the new, holy nature.

Here is why you still struggle with sin: "The desires of the flesh are against the Spirit, and the desires of the Spirit are against the flesh, for these are opposed to each other, to keep you from doing the things you want to do" (Galatians 5:17).
  • The flesh wants to do what?

  • The Spirit wants to do what?

  • Why is there such a conflict?

Can you relate to this battle Paul has been talking about? This is exactly what he's referring to in Galatians 5:17 when he says, "The desires of the flesh (*my sinful body*) are against the Spirit (*my new, holy nature*), and the desires of the Spirit are against the flesh, for these are opposed to each other, to keep you from doing the things you want to do."

In Romans 7, verses 17 through 19, Paul makes a very interesting declaration. He says, "It is no longer I (*my new, holy nature*) who do it *(who goes against God and sins)*, but sin that dwells within me. For I know that nothing good dwells in me, that is, in my flesh. For I *(my new, holy nature)* have the desire to do what is right, but not the ability to carry it out *(I struggle making my body do what God wants me to do)*. For I *(my new nature)* do not do *(daily behavior)* the good I *(my new nature)* want, but the evil *(sin)* I *(my new nature)* do not want is what I *(my flesh)* keep on doing."

This is war, my friend, plain and simple ... all-out-war!

Give it Some Thought
- Look again at the wording Paul uses in Romans 7:22-23 when he says that the inner being and the sinful flesh are at war. Did you notice where that war is taking place? Where is the battlefield?

- Why does the enemy want to attack your mind?

Week 11, Day 5

5. Ground Zero: My Mind
As we start today's study, I challenge you to consider carefully the following passage of Scripture. Every time you see the word "flesh" I want you to underline it. When you see the word "mind," circle it; and when you see the world "Spirit," draw a box around it.

> "For those who live according to the flesh set their minds on the things of the flesh, but those who live according to the Spirit set their minds on the things of the Spirit. For to set the mind on the flesh is death, but to set the mind on the Spirit is life and peace. For the mind that is set on the flesh is hostile to

God, for it does not submit to God's law; indeed, it cannot. Those who are in the flesh cannot please God. You, however, are not in the flesh but in the Spirit, if in fact the Spirit of God dwells in you. Anyone who does not have the Spirit of Christ does not belong to him. But if Christ is in you, although the body is dead because of sin, the Spirit is life because of righteousness. If the Spirit of him who raised Jesus from the dead dwells in you, he who raised Christ Jesus from the dead will also give life to your mortal bodies through his Spirit who dwells in you. So then, brothers, we are debtors, not to the flesh, to live according to the flesh. For if you live according to the flesh you will die, but if by the Spirit you put to death the deeds of the body, you will live. For all who are led by the Spirit of God are sons of God." (Romans 8:5-14)

- What role does your mind play in your relationship with God?

- Write out Isaiah 26:3 below.

When your mind is totally focused on God, when your thoughts are disciplined to think only on those things that are true, noble, right, pure, lovely, admirable, excellent and praiseworthy;[13] God promises to keep you in a place of safety—a place where you are able to experience an inner peace that is indescribable, and one that will stand guard over you at all times.[14]

This is why Satan's strategy is to attack your mind. He knows if he can impress your thinking, he will impact your living. "As water reflects the face, so one's life reflects the heart" (Proverbs 27:19). "Heart" in the Hebrew is the word "mind"; so, your behavior is a direct reflection of your thinking. When your mind is focused on living for

God, your decisions and actions will be more glorifying to God as well. So, to keep that from happening, the enemy is waging guerrilla warfare on your mind.

The greatest example we have of this is found in Genesis chapter three: the temptation of Eve. Paul speaks of that event with great fear —fear of what the enemy is capable of doing to each of us. "I am afraid that just as Eve was deceived by the serpent's cunning, your _minds_ may somehow be led astray from your sincere and pure devotion to Christ" (2 Corinthians 11:3 NIV '84, emphasis mine).

- Romans 13:14 commands us to "Clothe yourselves with the Lord Jesus Christ, and do not think about how to gratify the desires of the flesh." Why can't I _just think about_ satisfying my sinful desires?

Take a moment and read Romans 7:22-23. The battlefield is your mind, my friend. You must not—ever—allow your thoughts free reign. The result could be disastrous. Why? Because your sinful flesh is always pleading with your mind for satisfaction. It's relentless in its pursuit of sinful pleasures. This is why you're commanded to "destroy arguments and every lofty opinion raised against the knowledge of God, and _take every thought captive_ to obey Christ" (2 Corinthians 10:5, emphasis mine).

6. A Radical Transformation
There is one final text we must consider before we close out our study.
> "Do not conform any longer to the pattern of this world, but be _transformed_ by the _renewing of your mind_. Then you will be able to test and approve what God's will is—his good, pleasing and perfect will." (Romans 12:2 NIV '84, emphasis mine)

I like the word "transformed" here. It's the Greek word "metamorpho-o" from which we get our English word "metamorphosis." Can you remember science class in high school? A metamorphosis is a supernatural change that transforms something from one thing, into something totally different—completely unlike what it was before.

What makes a metamorphosis so unique is that the transformation takes place *from the inside out*! Oh, I gotta repeat that one. A metamorphosis is a supernatural change that happens from the inside out. In other words, when the metamorphosis is complete, that which was on the inside is now being lived out on the outside, thereby making you a totally different being from what you were before.

The reason a caterpillar transforms into a butterfly, as opposed to an earthworm becoming a butterfly, is because the caterpillar already has the nature of the butterfly inside of it. Once in the cocoon and the transition begins, the internal nature of the butterfly works its way out, totally transforming that caterpillar.

- Now, plug that back into Romans 12:2. We are to be "transformed." We are to undergo a spiritual metamorphosis. That which is on the inside is to be lived out on the outside. So, what is on the inside of every Christian? (Hint: see your diagram.)

What does that mean exactly? How does that impact or help me become God's Man of Steel? Let me share some Scripture here that will help you discover the answer.

"I am the Lord your God. Consecrate yourselves therefore, and *be holy*, for I am holy." (Leviticus 11:44)

"Speak to all the congregation of the people and say to them, You shall *be holy* for I the Lord your God am holy." (Leviticus 19:2)

"Consecrate yourselves, therefore, and *be holy*, for I am the Lord your God." (Leviticus 20:7)

"You shall *be holy*, for I am holy." 1 Peter 1:16

- According to these verses, what is it God expects us to be?

- Is that even possible? Can we ever be holy while here on earth?

Never forget, when God commands you to do something, no matter how impossible it might seem, with His power and through the leading of the Holy Spirit, you can do it. You can actually BE holy even as he is holy. But how? How can I possibly be holy when I struggle so much with sin?"

Look at your diagram again. It's vitally important that we not lose sight of the fact that God has already placed His holiness inside of you. Your new nature is a holy nature. You are Teknon Theos. You are a Super Man of God.

According to Romans 12:2, all you have to do to be transformed, to let that holiness which is "inside" of you be lived out on a daily basis —all you need to do to actually be a Super Man of God—is to renew your mind. Change the way you think!

> "Be *transformed* by the <u>renewing</u> of your mind." (Romans 12:2 NIV '84)

To "renew" is another word for renovate. When you are renovating a room or house, you always go through two major phases. First is demolition—you are gutting out all the old, leaving nothing behind. Second is remodeling—you are putting all brand new into the space vacated by the old.

It's the same thing with renovating your mind. To change the way you think, you must first gut the old way of thinking. That old way of thinking is centered around King Me. What will make me happy? What will bring me the most satisfaction and pleasure? All hail King Me. (See the diagram thought bubbles.)

That thought process needs to be gutted. Why? Remember, what I think strongly influences what I do. When I think about King Me, I will worship King Me. I will expect everyone and everything else to worship King Me as well. To be a Super Man of God you must get rid of that way of thinking. It's not about Me!

Once you've gutted out the old way of thinking, you then need to replace it with a brand new way of thinking: thinking that is centered on King Jesus. What will make God happy? What will bring Him the most honor and glory? All praise to King Jesus! (See the diagram thought bubbles.) Think about God and I will worship God.

- Read Romans 12:2 again: "Do not conform any longer to the pattern of this world, but be transformed by the renewing of your mind. Then you will be able to test and approve what God's will is—his good, pleasing and perfect will" (NIV '84). Here's a question for you: when I change the way I think; when I take my thoughts captive and make them obedient to Christ; when the focus of my heart is on glorifying God in everything I say and do … what is the final result?

Give it Some Thought
- Read these passages of Scripture. Under each passage, jot a note about how you can apply that text to the things you've learned in this study. Remember, our goal over the last 11 weeks wasn't just to complete another Bible study; it's to begin a lifelong process of change to BE the Super Man of God you were created to be. That begins with Scripture.

- Galatians 5:16-17

- Galatians 5:22-25

- 1 Thessalonians 4:4-5

- 1 Peter 4:2-3

- Galatians 6:7-8

- Romans 6:12-14

- 1 Corinthians 6:19-20

- Colossians 3:1-10

- 2 Corinthians 4:16

- Share with the guys at least one takeaway you received from this week, and what you plan to do about it.

"Finally, be strong in the Lord and in the strength of his might."
Ephesians 6:10

Not the End
We Can Do This!

God's Man of Steel

Pastor Rogers stood off to the side of the room, arms crossed over his chest, a tear running down his cheek, a massive smile beaming from ear to ear as he watched Mitch talk with a small group of men. It wasn't that long ago that Mitch was in his office, groaning over his failures to be a man of God. Now here he was, sharing his testimony with a group of men. Truly Mitch had become a Super Man of God!

"Guys," Mitch was saying, "you can do this! You can be God's man of steel! If God can change me, He can definitely change you!" Mitch paused for a moment, looking each man squarely in the eye before he continued. "Truth be told, I've learned that on my own I'm no Super Man. Shoot, on my own I kept messing things up. I thought I could be the man God wanted me to be, but every time I tried I'd blow it big-time!

"In this journey called life, God has taught me four very important truths." Mitch glanced over at Pastor Rogers and smiled. "If it weren't for my accountability partner, investing his time in patiently walking me through Scripture, praying for me—and with me; and, if it weren't for the power of God's Word at work in my life, I wouldn't be standing here right now telling you these things.

"So, as I close my time with you, I'd like to remind you of those four simple, yet life-changing truths I learned.

1. **You Are An Alien**
    Superman is an alien from another planet. No matter how

211

hard he tries to fit in, he cannot be like the world around him because he is not like the world around him.

As a born-again believer, you are also an alien. This world is not your home. No matter how hard you may try, you can never fit in to the world around you, because you're not like the world around you (see John 15:18-27; Matthew 10:22; 1 John 3:13).

Challenge: Embrace the fact that you are a stranger, a pilgrim, a foreigner in this wicked world and start living like the citizen of heaven you are! BE a Super Man of God!

2. **You Are a Super Man**
   Superman's supernatural powers come from his proximity to Earth's yellow sun. Without the sun he is weak, powerless over his archenemy who is trying to take him down.

   As a Super Man of God, you draw your strength to stand firm in the faith and resist the enemy from your proximity to God's Son. Without Christ, you can do nothing. Without Christ, you are powerless to stand against the archenemy of your soul.

   Challenge: Draw close to God. Make it your priority to invest time with Him DAILY. Be in the Word. Be on your knees in prayer. Be fully yielded to His Lordship in your life. BE a Super Man of God!

3. **Watch Out For Your Kryptonite**
   There is only one thing in the entire galaxy that can weaken Superman. Only one thing can sap him of his strength and make him vulnerable to the attacks of the enemy. That one thing is Kryptonite.

   Kryptonite is simply radiated chunks of Superman's past. Anytime he gets near a piece of Kryptonite, anytime he hangs around a piece of his past life, it gets between him and Earth's sun and it drains him of his strength.

   As a Super Man of God, there is only one thing that can sap you of your ability to stand firm in the faith, only one thing that can weaken you and make you vulnerable to your archenemy's attack. Your Kryptonite is your past: past habits, past choices, past thought patterns, past sins. When you choose to hang around and play around with your former life, your Kryptonite gets between you and God's Son.

Challenge: Stay strong and stay away from your Kryptonite. BE a Super Man of God!

4. **Take Off Your Costume**

What makes Superman special among the long list of comic book superheroes is that Kal-El doesn't have to put on a costume to become Superman. He is always the man of steel. He never ceases to be Superman.

In an effort to "fit in" with the world around him, in an attempt to blend in so as not to be noticed, in his struggle to be accepted by his peers, Superman puts on the costume of Clark Kent. But that's not who he really is.

As a born-again believer, you ARE a Super Man of God. That's not a costume you have to put on. It's not a persona you have to try to manufacture. It's who you are. But more than likely, you are wearing a costume: not a superhero costume, but an average Joe costume. Our tendency is to shy away from being a Super Man of God so that we can fit in with the rest of the world. We tend to want to blend in instead of stand out.

"Guys, I challenge you to remove the costume. Rip open your proverbial shirt and reveal *the real you* to the world around you. BE a Super Man of God!"

References

Adventures of Superman. Superman Inc. 1952-1958.

The Bible. New International Version, Zondervan, 1984.

The Bible. New King James Version, Thomas Nelson, 1982.

The English Standard Version Bible. Crossway, 2001.

Evans, Tony. *Life Essentials*. Chicago: Moody Publishers, 2007. p. 135.

Gladiator. Directed by Ridley Scott. DreamWorks SKG, Universal Pictures, Scott Free Productions, 2000.

"The Howling Man." *Twilight Zone*. Written by Charles Beaumont and Rod Serling, directed by Douglas Heyes. Columbia Broadcast System (CBS), 4 Nov. 1960.

Lord of the Rings: The Fellowship of the Ring. Directed by Peter Jackson. New Line Cinema, Wing Nut Films, 2001.

Milne, A. A. *Winnie-the-Pooh*. NY: Dutton Children's Books, 1926. Redesigned 1988.

Mote, Edward. "My Hope is Built on Nothing Less." c. 1834. Composed by John Stainer, 1873.

Smallville Wiki. Web. 2017. <http://smallville.wikia.com/wiki/Fortress_of_Solitude>

Star Wars: Episode V – The Empire Strikes Back. Directed by Irvin Kershner, with performances by Mark Hamill, Harrison Ford, Carrie Fisher. Lucasfilm, 1980.

Star Wars: Episode VI – Return of The Jedi. Directed by Richard Marquand, with performances by Mark Hamill, Harrison Ford, Carrie Fisher. Lucasfilm, 1983.

About the Author

Steve Etner is a national men's speaker. Through the Pure Man Ministry, Steve coaches men across the globe, sharing God's truth in such a way as to help guys become men of godliness, purity and integrity. Steve has authored *Extreme Mind Makeover: How to transform thoughts and habits into God-pleasing patterns* and *The Pure Man's Devotional Guide: A biblical toolbox for purity*. He and his wife, Heather, live in Granger, Indiana.

About Overboard Ministries

Overboard Books is the publishing arm of Overboard Ministries, whose mission is based on Matthew 14. In that chapter we find the familiar story of Jesus walking on water while His disciples were in a boat. It was the middle of the night, the water was choppy and Jesus freaked out His followers who thought He was a ghost. When they realized it was Him, Peter asked to come out to Him on the water, and he actually walked on top of the water like Jesus.

But what truly captivates me is the thought of the other eleven disciples who remained in the boat. I've often wondered how many of them questioned that move in the years to come? How many of them wished they hadn't stayed in the boat but had instead gone overboard with Peter? Overboard Ministries aims to help Christians get out of the boat and live life out on the water with Christ. We hope and pray that each book published by Overboard Ministries will stir believers to jump overboard and live life all-out for God, full of joy and free from the regret of "I wish I had…"

What we do
Overboard Ministries emerged in the Spring of 2011 as an umbrella ministry for several concepts my wife and I were developing. One of those concepts was a book ministry that would help other Christian authors get published. I experienced a lot of frustration while passing my first manuscript around. I kept getting rejection letters that were kindly written, but each echoed the same sentiment: "We love this book. If you were already a published author, we would love to publish it." They were nice letters, but that didn't make the rejection any easier or the logic less frustrating.

Out of that came the audacious idea to start our own "publishing company." I put that in quotes because I want people to know a couple of things. First of all, we're not a traditional publishing company like most people envision when they hear the name. We don't have a printing press in our garage, and we don't have a marketing team. Basically, we're a middle-man who absorbs most of the cost of publishing in order to help you get published, while making sure the majority of profits end up in your pocket, not ours.

Our desire is to keep costs to a bare minimum for each author. (As of this writing, there is only a minimal contract fee when your manuscript is accepted.) We provide resources and ideas to help authors work on marketing, while also providing the editor and graphic design artist at our expense. We subcontract out the printing, which speeds up the time it takes to move from final draft to bound book. Since we don't have much overhead we can keep our expenses low, allowing seasoned authors, or first-time authors like me, the opportunity to profit from their writing.

Contact us

If you are interested in other books or learning about other authors from Overboard Books, please visit our website at www.overboardministries.com and click on the "Store" link. If you are an author interested in publishing with us, please visit our site and check out the "Authors" tab. There you will find a wealth of information that will help you understand the publishing process and how we might be a good fit for you. If we're not a fit for you, we'll gladly share anything we've learned that might be helpful to you as you pursue publishing through other means.

Thank you

Thanks for supporting our work and ministry. If you believe this book was helpful to you, tell someone about it! Or better yet, buy them a copy of their own! We completely depend on word-of-mouth grassroots marketing to help spread the word about Overboard Ministries and its publications. Please share our website with others and encourage them to purchase the materials that will help them live "overboard" lives for Christ.

May God bless you as you grab the side of boat, take a deep breath…and jump onto the sea!

Joe Castañeda
Founder, Overboard Ministries

End Notes

Chapter 1

1. Isaiah 43:7. Compare with 1 Corinthians 10:31; Colossians 3:17; and 1 Peter 4:11.
2. Colossians 3:17
3. 1 Corinthians 10:31
4. Genesis 1:26; Psalm 95:6, 100:3, 139:14; Isaiah 54:5 and John 1:3
5. Jeremiah 15:16
6. 1 Peter 2:2
7. 1 Timothy 4:7-8; 1 Corinthians 9:27; 2 Peter 3:11
8. 1 Timothy 4:7

Chapter 2

1. Philippians 4:13
2. John 15:5
3. Joshua 1:6,9; Deuteronomy 31:6
4. James 4:7
5. Edmund Burke (1729–1797) was a British statesman and influential political thinker.
6. See 1 Samuel 15
7. 1 Samuel 15:26
8. 1 Samuel 16:7
9. 1 Samuel 16:11-12
10. Acts 13:22
11. 1 Samuel 17:1-54
12. 1 Samuel 18:5
13. 1 Samuel 18:6-8
14. 1 Samuel 22:2
15. *Gladiator*. Directed by Ridley Scott. DreamWorks SKG, Universal Pictures, Scott Free Productions, 2000.
16. 2 Samuel 23:10
17. Psalm 108:13; compare with 1 Corinthians 15:57
18. Philippians 4:13; 2 Peter 1:3

19. *Lord of the Rings: The Fellowship of the Ring*. Directed by Peter Jackson. New Line Cinema, Wing Nut Films, 2001.
20. 2 Samuel 23:11-12

Chapter 3

1. *Smallville Wiki*. Web. 2017. <http://smallville.wikia.com/wiki/Fortress_of_Solitude>
2. Philippians 3:20
3. John 15:18-19; Matthew 10:22
4. Genesis 4:7
5. Matthew 6:33; 1 Corinthians 10:31; Colossians 3:17
6. 2 Timothy 2:19
7. Isaiah 28:16
8. Matthew 6:19-20
9. 1 Corinthians 3:11; compare with Isaiah 28:16
10. Mote, Edward. "My Hope is Built on Nothing Less." c. 1834. Composed by John Stainer, 1873.
11. Psalm 118:22; Luke 20:17; Ephesians 2:20
12. Hebrews 4:12
13. 2 Timothy 3:16-17
14. Luke 11:28; compare with Psalm 1:1-3; 112:1; Proverbs 8:32
15. Psalm 18:30; compare with Psalm 12:6; 2 Samuel 22:31; Proverbs 30:5
16. Psalm 119:105; 2 Peter 1:19
17. Romans 15:4
18. Joshua 1:8
19. Psalm 19:7-9
20. 1 Peter 2:2
21. Isaiah 40:8; Matthew 24:35
22. Psalm 119:4
23. Psalm 119:9
24. Psalm 119:66
25. Psalm 119:98
26. Psalm 119:99
27. Psalm 119:105, 130
28. John 16:13
29. Luke 6:48

30. 1 Peter 2:6-7

Chapter 4
1. Evans, Tony. *Life Essentials*. Chicago: Moody Publishers, 2007. p 135.
2. 1 Peter 2:2; 1 Corinthians 3:2; and Hebrews 5:12-13
3. Milne, A. A. *Winnie-the-Pooh*. NY: Dutton Children's Books, 1926. Redesigned 1988.
4. Proverbs 4:23

Chapter 5
1. John 1:12; compare with 1 John 3:1 and Romans 8:14-17
2. John 1:12; compare with Acts 4:12; 16:31 and Galatians 3:26
3. Matthew 5:14-16
4. Revelation 1:6, 4:11, 5:12
5. Compare with Romans 16:27; Ephesians 4:21; 1 Timothy 1:17 and Jude 25
6. Revelation 21:6, 22:13; Isaiah 44:6, 48:12
7. Isaiah 40:26, 28; John 1:3, 10; 1 Corinthians 8:6 and Colossians 1:16
8. Revelation 1:4, 8
9. Exodus 34:6; compare with Exodus 22:27; Nehemiah 9:27; Psalm 51:1, 86:15, 103:8, 111:4, 116:5, 119:156, 145:8; and Isaiah 63:7
10. Hebrews 5:9, 12:2
11. John 6:32, 35
12. 2 Corinthians 1:4, 7:6-7; Isaiah 49:13, 51:12, 66:13
13. Isaiah 9:6, 28:29
14. Matthew 21:42; Mark 12:10; Ephesians 2:20 and 1 Peter 2:6
15. Ephesians 1:17
16. James 1:17 and 1 John 1:5
17. John 17:25
18. Psalm 68:5
19. John 14:6; compare with John 10:8; Ephesians 2:18; Hebrews 10:20; John 1:4; 11:25
20. 1 Timothy 1:17
21. Psalm 80:7

22. Psalm 18:46; compare with Isaiah 17:10, 61:10; Psalm 18:46, 66:5, 68:19; Habakkuk 3:18; Luke 1:47; 1 Timothy 1:1; 2:3; 4:10
23. 2 Corinthians 1:3-4; compare with Psalm 23:4, 71:21, 86:17; Isaiah 12:1, 49:13
24. 1 Peter 5:10
25. Hebrews 4:16; Ephesians 2:4-5; compare with Deuteronomy 4:31 and Nehemiah 9:31
26. Romans 16:20 and 1 Thessalonians 5:23
27. Jeremiah 51:56
28. Psalm 31:5; compare with Isaiah 45:19, 65:16 and John 14:6
29. Genesis 16:13 and Psalm 139:1-12
30. Psalm 99:8; compare with Psalm 32:5, 51:2; 1 John 1:9 and Ephesians 1:7
31. Psalm 18:47-48
32. Genesis 17:1, 28:3, 35:11, 43:14; Exodus 6:3 and 2 Samuel 5:10
33. Psalm 147:5; Isaiah 40:28; Jeremiah 23:24; 1 John 3:20 and Hebrews 4:13
34. Psalm 147:5; Job 42:2; Isaiah 44:24; Matthew 19:26; Mark 10:27; Luke 1:37 and Romans 1:20
35. Psalm 139:1-24; Proverbs 15:3; Isaiah 66:1; Jeremiah 23:23-24 and Colossians 1:17
36. Hebrews 3:4
37. Amos 4:13; compare with Psalm 65:6, 135:7
38. Isaiah 43:25; compare with 2 Samuel 12:13; Mark 2:7; Luke 5:21 and Acts 3:19
39. Isaiah 51:12
40. Matthew 2:2, 27:11; John 18:39 and Revelation 15:3
41. Jeremiah 10:7; compare with Psalm 22:28; Revelation 15:4
42. Psalm 47:2, 95:3, 97:9
43. Daniel 4:37
44. Psalm 24:7-8; compare with Psalm 29:3; Acts 7:2 and 1 Corinthians 2:8
45. 1 Timothy 6:15; Revelation 19:16; compare with Deuteronomy 10:17; Psalm 136:3; Daniel 2:47, 4:26; Revelation 1:5, 17:14
46. Psalm 44:4, 74:12

47. Revelation 15:3
48. Psalm 7:17
49. Psalm 115:15, 121:2 and Joshua 3:13
50. Psalm 59:11; compare with Psalm 3:3, 5:12, 18:2, 28:7, 33:20, 119:114; Genesis 15:1; Deuteronomy 33:29 and 2 Samuel 22:3, 31
51. Joshua 24:24
52. Psalm 95:6 and Isaiah 51:13
53. Jeremiah 23:6, 33:16
54. 1 Corinthians 2:8 and James 2:1
55. Judges 6:24; 2 Thessalonians 3:16 and Romans 16:33
56. Matthew 9:38
57. Deuteronomy 10:17; 1 Timothy 6:15; Revelation 17:14, 19:16
58. Colossians 3:11
59. 2 Samuel 22:2-3; Psalm 18:2; compare with 1 Samuel 2:2; Deuteronomy 32:4; Psalm 28:7, 31:3, 33:20, 71:3-4, 91:2, 144:2
60. John 20:17
61. Psalm 27:9, 33:20, 40:17, 46:1
62. Psalm 32:7
63. Psalm 25:5, 71:5; compare with Psalm 33:20, 39:7, 42:5
64. Job 19:25; Psalm 19:14, 23:11, 78:35; Isaiah 41:14, 47:4
65. See James 1:13
66. *Star Wars: Episode V – The Empire Strikes Back*. Directed by Irvin Kershner, with performances by Mark Hamill, Harrison Ford, Carrie Fisher. Lucasfilm, 1980.
67. *Adventures of Superman*. Superman Inc. 1952-1958.
68. Romans 15:4 and 1 Corinthians 10:11-12
69. 1 Peter 4:11
70. Isaiah 43:7; compare with Romans 11:36; 1 Corinthians 8:6; 11:12; Colossians 1:16; John 1:3 and Hebrews 2:10
71. 1 Corinthians 10:31; compare with Psalm 86:12; Ecclesiastes 12:13; Colossians 3:17 and Revelation 4:11
72. Philippians 2:5-8; James 4:7, 10 and 1 Peter 5:6-10
73. Psalm 119:30; Luke 6:46; John 14:15, 31; and Acts 5:29
74. Colossians 3:17
75. Psalm 139:4; compare with Matthew 12:36-37; Ephesians 4:29; Psalm 19:14 and James 1:26

76. Luke 1:37, 18:27
77. 1 John 5:3
78. Isaiah 32:6
79. Ecclesiastes 12:14
80. Luke 12:2-3
81. 1 Corinthians 4:5

Chapter 6
1. Exodus 7:25
2. Exodus 7:20-21
3. Exodus 7:24
4. Exodus 7:21
5. Exodus 8:6
6. Exodus 8:7
7. Exodus 8:9
8. Exodus 8:10
9. Genesis 35:2
10. Deuteronomy 6:14; compare with Exodus 23:13 and Isaiah 44:6
11. James 1:13
12. James 1:14
13. Philippians 4:13
14. Ephesians 4:27
15. 2 Corinthians 10:5
16. James 1:15
17. Hebrews 11:25
18. Romans 6:14
19. Philippians 4:13
20. 2 Peter 1:3

Chapter 7
1. Ephesians 6:12
2. Proverbs 27:19
3. Ephesians 1:5; John 1:12; Galatians 4:5-6; and Romans 8:15-17
4. Titus 3:7
5. Deuteronomy 31:6, 8; 1 Chronicles 28:20; Psalm 37:28, 94:14
6. James 4:7

7. Deuteronomy 20:3-4
8. Hebrews 13:8; Malachi 3:6; James 1:17; and Psalm 90:2
9. 2 Peter 1:3 and 1 Samuel 17:47
10. Philippians 4:19
11. Matthew 4:1-11 and Luke 4:1-13
12. Philippians 4:13
13. 2 Peter 1:3
14. Philippians 2:13

Chapter 8

1. Genesis 13:5-11
2. Genesis 19
3. Acts 16:31
4. Ephesians 2:8-9
5. Galatians 5:17; 2 Peter 2:7-8
6. Ecclesiastes 12:13
7. Proverbs 27:19
8. 2 Peter 2:7-8
9. Matthew 6:33
10. Genesis 19:1
11. Genesis 19:7
12. Genesis 19:8
13. Genesis 19:14
14. Genesis 19:16
15. Genesis 19:26
16. Genesis 19:33-36
17. 2 Peter 2:8
18. Ephesians 5:15-17
19. Matthew 5:28
20. Psalm 119:37
21. Psalm 101:2-3
22. Matthew 13:22
23. Proverbs 4:25
24. Psalm 141:8
25. Joshua 1:7; Deuteronomy 28:14; and Joshua 23:6

Chapter 9

1. Okay, I need to make sure I didn't offend anyone by stating that those superheroes and archvillains aren't real people. But

hey, dude, if you believe they truly exist you might want to set up a meeting with your pastor!

2. Job 1:6-12, 2:1-7
3. Revelation 9:11
4. John 10:10
5. 2 Corinthians 2:11
6. *Star Wars: Episode VI – Return of The Jedi*. Directed by Richard Marquand, with performances by Mark Hamill, Harrison Ford, Carrie Fisher. Lucasfilm, 1983.
7. 2 Corinthians 11:3
8. 2 Corinthians 10:5
9. Philippians 4:8
10. 2 Timothy 3:16-17
11. 1 John 5:3-4
12. Deuteronomy 4:2, 12:32; and Proverbs 30:6
13. "The Howling Man." *Twilight Zone*. Written by Charles Beaumont and Rod Serling, directed by Douglas Heyes. Columbia Broadcast System (CBS), 4 Nov. 1960.
14. Genesis 1:26-27

Chapter 10
1. Daniel 1:6; Belteshazzar means "Bel protects his life."
2. Daniel 2:1-49
3. Daniel 1:6
4. Daniel 2:49
5. Daniel 3:8-18
6. Daniel 6:4
7. Daniel 6:6-9
8. Daniel 6:10
9. Daniel 6:16
10. Daniel 6:20-21
11. 1 Thessalonians 4:1
12. 1 Peter 1:14
13. Ephesians 5:8
14. Matthew 5:14
15. Matthew 5:15-16
16. 2 Corinthians 7:1
17. Philippians 3:20
18. 2 Peter 1:3
19. James 4:7
20. Galatians 5:16; 1 Corinthians 10:13; Ephesians 6:10-18

21. James 4:4; Romans 12:2; 1 John 2:15-16
22. Ephesians 6:12
23. 2 Corinthians 11:3
24. Ephesians 1:5; John 1:12; Galatians 4:5-6; and Romans 8:15-17
25. Titus 3:7
26. Deuteronomy 31:6, 8; 1 Chronicles 28:20; Psalm 37:28 and 94:14
27. Philippians 4:13, 19
28. 1 Samuel 17
29. Hebrews 13:8; Malachi 3:6; James 1:17; and Psalm 90:2
30. 2 Peter 1:3; 1 Samuel 17:47

Chapter 11

1. Romans 8:27
2. 1 Peter 5:8-9; James 4:7
3. Romans 7:22
4. Psalm 51:6
5. Ephesians 3:16
6. Romans 8:3; Matthew 26:41; and 2 Corinthians 4:16
7. Romans 7:15-25
8. Ephesians 2:1, 5
9. Ephesians 2:12
10. Galatians 5:16
11. Habakkuk 1:13
12. Psalm 5:4-5, 101:7; Habakkuk 1:13
13. Philippians 4:8
14. Philippians 4:7

65773263R00133

Made in the USA
Lexington, KY
24 July 2017